"There is no such thing as 'diaconal' preaching, as distinct from presbyteral or lay preaching. But, as Cormier notes, there is a way in which the distinct experiences of the deacon—as a man of service among the marginalized—should shape his preaching. Using an abundance of clear and simple examples, mostly drawn from his own preaching, Cormier illuminates that way. Cormier shows how the deacon can 'pass his life through the fire of thought' in order to speak a relevant word for ordinary folk struggling to make sense of the Gospel in daily life."

—Ann M. Garrido
Associate Professor of Homiletics
Aquinas Institute of Theology

"What is abundantly clear in *The Deacon's Ministry of the Word* is that its author, Jay Cormier, not only understands the art of communication but is a gifted communicator. With clarity and conciseness, with bundles of examples and engaging images, he lays out a vision of preaching that is spot on target. What a gift to the preaching community."

—Robert F. Morneau
Auxiliary Bishop Emeritus of Green Bay
Pastor of Resurrection Parish

The Deacon's Ministry of the Word

Jay Cormier

LITURGICAL PRESS
Collegeville, Minnesota

www.litpress.org

1   2   3   4   5   6   7   8   9

Library of Congress Cataloging-in-Publication Data

Names: Cormier, Jay, author.
Title: The deacon's ministry of the word / by Jay Cormier.
Description: Collegeville, Minnesota : Liturgical Press, 2016. | Series: The deacon's ministry
Identifiers: LCCN 2016007174 (print) | LCCN 2016023780 (ebook) | ISBN 9780814648223 (pbk.) | ISBN 9780814648476 (ebook)
Subjects: LCSH: Preaching. | Deacons.
Classification: LCC BV4211.3 .C67 2016 (print) | LCC BV4211.3 (ebook) | DDC 251—dc23
LC record available at https://lccn.loc.gov/2016007174

For Ann

Contents

Preface

When first presented with the idea of writing this book, I must confess a certain reluctance in taking it on.

A book for deacons on preaching?

Effective preaching is the result of the same reflection, planning, and plain hard work whether the homilist is a bishop, priest, or deacon. There is no such thing as "priest preaching" and "deacon preaching"—or even "lay preaching." The homily is either inspiring or vacuous; it either reveals the love of God in our midst or befuddles or bores its hearers; it either works or it doesn't. I was skeptical of trying to write a book on preaching designed specifically for deacons.

But after many years of teaching speech communications and giving workshops on preaching (as well as from my own work as a deacon), I've come to realize that ministers come to homiletics from very different backgrounds, experiences, and expectations. So, despite my initial reluctance, I was pushed on by the good folk at Liturgical Press, and so you now hold this book in your hands.

As advertised and titled, this book primarily has the deacon in mind, especially those who are taking their first tentative steps in preaching. But it is my hope that anyone who has the courage and generosity of heart and spirit to proclaim the Word of God will find some useful ideas and approaches in these pages. While the writing and delivery of the Sunday homily are front and center, the strategies here can be applied to any proclamation of the Word in any number of formats and venues (by ordained and non-ordained alike).

A word about the layout of this book: The material is presented in the form of eight chapters or "essays." While there is a certain logic to the order in which they appear in the book, the essays do not have to be read in sequence. Readers may find a particular essay especially helpful as they develop their own strengths or are working on a particular skill at a given time. Each chapter/essay has been written to stand alone; to that end, some ideas are repeated from chapter to chapter for context and continuity.

Each chapter ends with a section titled *Communicare* (pronounced co-mune-i-KAH-ray), the Latin word that is the root of *communications*: "to make common." These sections offer practical suggestions and exercises for incorporating the ideas of that essay into your own preaching ministry.

This book is the latest of several projects I have been privileged to be a part of for Liturgical Press. My thanks to Barry Hudock and the skilled and conscientious editors in Collegeville for the invitation to contribute to this series of resources for deacons and for their encouragement and guidance in writing this book. I am grateful, as well, to my colleagues at Saint Anselm College—a special word of thanks to Dr. Sherry Shepler, coordinator of the college's Communications Studies program, who generously provided her counsel along the way.

The material here has been honed over the years in courses and workshops I have led for priests, deacons, and ministers, both in my home Diocese of Manchester, New Hampshire, and around the country. I am grateful to all who participated in those sessions—I assure you all that I learned as much from you as you did from me, and this book reflects a great deal of what you taught me.

The homilies appearing in the book are mostly from sermons I have preached at Saints Mary and Joseph Parish in Salem, New Hampshire, where I serve as deacon. My thanks to Rev. John Michalowski, SJ, to the Jesuit priests who serve at our parish, and to our parish community for their encouragement and counsel.

Two of the essays here began life as contributions to other publications. The chapter on preaching "visually" first appeared in *Worship* ("Preaching Visually: Helping Your Community 'See' God in Their Midst," September 2012, vol. 86, no. 5). I will be forever grateful to the late Rev. R. Kevin Seasoltz, OSB, for shepherding the original piece, which has been updated for this book.

The final chapter on the spirituality of the preacher is an expanded version of an essay that was published in the journal *Church*, published by the National Pastoral Life Center ("Emerson's Portrait of the Preacher," Summer 2007, vol. 23, no. 2). The work of the late Msgr. Philip Murnion was a prophetic gift to the American church; both he and the center he founded are sorely missed.

And my thanks, as always, to my most critical editor, my best friend, my beloved spouse, Ann. Her wisdom and skill made this manuscript a better book; her compassion and care make its author a better person.

May the pages that follow serve as a useful tool to you in your call to proclaim God's word of reconciling love in your midst.

CHAPTER 1

Morning Drive

It's 7:45 on a weekday morning. Thousands of cars, buses, and trains stream into the city of Boston from the Massachusetts North Shore, the Cape, and Southern New Hampshire, while another endless queue of vehicles heads to the technology companies along Route 128 that loops around the city to the north and west.

The commuters riding in all of these cars and buses and trains are plugged into any number of internet sites and radio stations. One of the most listened-to is Boston's all-news station, with its format of information, weather, and those all-important traffic reports.

On this particular morning, between the business news headlines and a report on another fender bender on a major thoroughfare, listeners to the all-news station hear this simple message, spoken by a warm, friendly female voice:

> My ear surgeon at Mass. Eye and Ear used a new technique
> to restore Mozart's *Clarinet Concerto*.
> He's also done wonders for the goldfinches in my backyard,
> and, using his skill and experience,
> he gave me back my husband's bad jokes.

The next hour, listeners heard the following, voiced by a middle-aged husband:

> My eye surgeon at Mass. Eye and Ear
> completely restored my wife's beautiful smile.

He also corrected our Friday nights
with old black-and-white movies
and gave me back the sunrise over Boston Harbor.

Two other spots were part of this radio campaign: one featured a mom
telling the story of her daughter, a ballet student:

The pediatric specialists at Mass. Eye and Ear
worked wonders for our daughter's recurring ear infection.
They also restored her ballet rehearsals on Tuesday nights
and gave her back her pink tutu she never wants to take off.

And, in the fourth spot, a little girl tells what the hospital did for her
beloved grandmother:

The really good doctors as Mass. Eye and Ear helped my
    grandmother
with the princesses and dragons in my storybook.
They did something to fix her eyes
so she could come visit us more often and read my favorite stories.

Mass. Eye and Ear is one of Boston's many world-class hospitals. The
hospital recently expanded its number of clinics in the suburbs north
and west of the city. As part of its communications campaign to increase its presence in the Boston area, Mass. Eye and Ear designed
these commercials that aired on several Boston radio stations.

Plugging In

The design, writing, and execution of these radio commercials do
all the right things in terms of smart, effective communications
strategizing.

First, the hospital focused on *a single, clear message*: Mass. Eye and
Ear can help restore the quality of life of anyone experiencing vision
and hearing problems. The point is not to sing the praises of the hospital; the expertise of the doctors, though impressive, and the state-
of-the-art technology of the facility are not what matters to the listener.
What matters is what that expertise and technology can do for *you*,
how Mass. Eye and Ear can improve and enhance the quality of *your*
life: enabling you to hear again the beauty of Mozart and the joy of

finches; correcting your clarity of vision to behold the beauty of your spouse's smile, your favorite movies, and a sunrise over the ocean; restoring your child's sense of balance so that she can dance again; improving your eyesight to enjoy those special moments of reading to your grandchild.

In other words, these four ads are *not* about Mass. Eye and Ear. They're about *you*.

And there are no secondary "messages" that distract from that primary message—nothing about the credentials of the hospital, no appeals to donate to the hospital foundation. True, focusing on one principal idea is also dictated by the fact that each ad is only thirty seconds in length. But the singular focus—how Mass. Eye and Ear can matter to *you*—makes the ads effective.

The hospital *engages the audience* in the spots by using images and language that listeners recognize from their own experience. The ads "speak" to their intended audience in words and ideas that they know and can comprehend, that evoke meaning to them, that matter to them. No ponderous medical jargon or forbidding technological wizardry is heard in these short messages. The writers of these commercials understand what the hospital services can mean to the everyday lives of patients—and subtly challenge them to move beyond their fears of doctors and hospitals in order to see the good that can result. The listeners *are* the wife, the husband, the mom, and the granddaughter telling their stories here. Their stories *are* the listeners' stories.

Note, too, that these ads are addressed to a specific, well-defined audience: parents of young children and middle-aged and late-middle-aged adults who are concerned about issues of health and quality of life. The ads' creators know when and how to reach these folks: Mass. Eye and Ear bought time on a radio station that their intended audience listens to—the all-news station. The ads' creators also realize that, although all-news stations may have smaller audience numbers than most music stations, listeners are actively engaged in listening to news programming: they're paying far more attention to what is being said on all-news stations than listeners to other radio formats. And they also bought time when that audience would most likely be listening: morning "drive time" when they're on their way to work.

The ads *engender the audience's trust*. Mass. Eye and Ear is one of many excellent hospitals in the northeast; its reputation is sterling. But it can also be daunting for many people who have never been seriously ill or who only know Mass. Eye and Ear as one of those mammoth medical complexes in downtown Boston. So the hospital has to present itself as *approachable*. The voices in these commercials do that.

The "first" voice in each of the four commercials is the parent, the spouse, the granddaughter, and the woman who clearly appreciates life. Listeners "trust" these voices and come to like them—because these are the audience's voices, telling the audience's stories. They speak of hope and possibility beyond whatever medical issues the listener might be facing.

A second "voice" concludes each commercial: a professional announcer's voice that possesses an appealing combination of warmth and authority. This voice invites listeners:

> When hearing problems affect the way you experience life,
> experience the difference Mass. Eye and Ear can make.
> We offer a full range of truly world-class ear, eye, nose, face, and
>   throat services
> at more than a dozen locations in the Boston area
> to help you experience life.
> Visit MassEyeandEar.org for more information.

> [Or:]

> Vision problems don't affect your eyes;
> they keep you from experiencing other parts of life that are
>   important.
> At Mass. Eye and Ear,
> we offer a full range of truly world-class ear, eye, nose, face, and
>   throat services
> at more than a dozen locations in the Boston area
> to help you experience life.
> Visit MassEyeandEar.org for more information.[1]

The tone and content of the four spots establish Mass. Eye and Ear as more than an excellent medical facility: they make its services a real possibility for listeners to consider, a place that no longer seems distant or remote but welcoming and approachable.

Finally, each of the Mass. Eye and Ear spots invites *a clear and specific response from the listener*. Humans communicate in order to affect another human being's behavior. We reach out to another person in words and pictures in order to get that other human being to *do* something: to buy, to support, to attend. Humans communicate in order to warn, to entice, to counsel, to reach agreement.

An effective message makes clear how the audience should respond—and how that response is in their best interests. Better, still, if the response sought is as easy as possible. The announcer's closing line in each of the four ads does exactly that: after encouraging listeners to imagine how the services of Mass. Eye and Ear might enhance the quality of their lives, the ads direct them to visit the hospital's (easy-to-remember) website for more information on how they can begin to realize those possibilities.

Communications—whether a radio commercial, a classroom lecture, a sales presentation, or a news report from the scene of some catastrophic event—is a *system*. Messages are successfully sent because the various elements in the system work together to elicit the intended response and action. The Mass. Eye and Ear radio commercials mirror that model:

- a clear, focused, believable message is sent to a specific target audience, appealing to their interests, needs, and problems;

- the message is articulated in a language (or "code")—pictures, stories, music—that the audience will understand and respond to, and "transmitted" through a "channel" that this particular audience is plugged into and engaged with;

- the sender of the message presents himself or herself as worthy of trust: that he or she is empathetic, understanding, approachable, and *likable*; and

- the audience is made to understand how responding to the message is in their best interests.

Communicare

The same factors and realities that the writers and producers of the Mass. Eye and Ear radio commercials considered when they developed these spots are the same factors and realities that should be considered by any individual or group seeking to communicate a message that will be embraced by an intended audience.

In proclaiming the Word of God in whatever place or time, preachers and teachers are engaged, first, in a system of communications. The word *communications* comes from the Latin word *communicare* (pronounced co-mune-i-KAH-ray)—to "make common." It comes from the same root as another important word in our tradition: *communion.*

This book is about the deacon's ministry of proclaiming the Word of God. In the deacon's ministry, such proclamation takes place in a number of venues: the church, the classroom, the living room, sometimes even the local tavern. The deacon speaks that Word to the many different constituencies that make up a parish—parents, children, teenagers, young singles, seniors—and different groups with a myriad of special interests and concerns: baptismal catechesis for parents, gospel exegesis to RCIA groups, marriage preparation for engaged couples, reports to finance committees. As a minister of the Word, the deacon is sometimes the homilist, but different needs and times in every parish call the deacon to serve as the teacher, the guide, the counselor, the arbiter, the advocate. And most deacons have been called upon to speak God's Word in places and circumstances they never imagined.

The pages that follow focus on what can best be described as *strategizing* the proclamation of God's Word: planning, designing, and executing that proclamation before a given audience, in a particular setting, under a unique set of circumstances. As expected, a principal focus here will be the Sunday homily, the liturgical setting where deacons are most often called upon to proclaim the Word. But the communications strategies discussed here can be employed by deacons (and priests and laity as well) in any number of ministerial situations in which they help an individual or group encounter the Word of God: from a retreat day for dads in the parish to a budget presentation to the parish council.

The same intellectual and creative process that Mass. Eye and Ear employed to develop its radio ads to increase visibility in their community are the same strategies that deacons can employ in the Sunday homily or in any presentation. Each strategy will be developed in the essays that make up this book, but let's begin with a quick overview of the strategies employed so effectively by Mass. Eye and Ear:

Focus on One Central Point

Every effective presentation has a focal point: a single, clear idea that the presenter wants the audience to "get." It may be a particular response or action the presenter wants the audience to do; it may be to help the audience understand a situation in a new way; it may be to obtain the audience's assent or approval for the first step in a complex process or on-going project.

As noted above, every communication seeks to affect another person's behavior:

"Be careful of the wet paint."

"Use the right sunscreen before going outside."

"You'll grow more beautiful, healthier plants if you use this fertilizer."

"Your support will help us find a cure."

"Begin by inserting piece A into slot B."

"God loves you even though you're not too crazy about yourself at the moment."

So what's the one idea you want your audience to take away from this Sunday's gospel? What's the most important concept you need to make the committee understand as they move forward? What single notion do you want the retreatants to take home with them from your conference?

The Mass. Eye and Ear radio spots focused on how the hospital's services could make better the everyday lives of the hearers of the message. The effective proclamation of God's Word in whatever format is similarly centered on a single idea.

Engage the Audience

"Engaging" the audience is not about entertaining them.

To engage the audience is to make them see how what you are talking about *matters* to them. Mass. Eye and Ear made listeners understand how their facility and the care it provides can and should *matter* to them.

What matters to us engages us. What we perceive as important, what we understand as in our interests, what we see as a clear benefit to us doesn't bore us.

So engaging the audience begins in the reality and experience of those you are talking with.

Engender Trust

Why should the community listen to *you*? Can you speak with credibility about this subject? Do you understand where the audience is coming from and why they think as they do regarding this issue—why they are predisposed to your position and why they might be hostile? Are you perceived as competent, approachable, *likable*?

To put it more bluntly: Do you *walk the talk*?

Prayer is central here—spending time quietly discerning what God is calling you to do as a deacon as you struggle every day to fulfill your ordination call to be a "herald" of the Gospel of Christ: "Believe what you read, teach what you believe, and practice what you teach."

Trust begins with humility: humility that is centered in respect for those served. Such humility is communicated principally in the tone and attitude, the sincerity and empathy, that listeners perceive in the preacher/teacher.

Inspire Action and Change

There is no greater failure in communications than an audience saying at the end of a presentation, *What was that about?*

The goal of communications is action. What do you want the person or persons you are engaging to *do*? What response do you want from them? Sometimes the response you seek may be very specific and clear: support my cause, vote for my candidate, buy my product. Other times, an immediate reaction may be sought: to laugh, to cry, to applaud (when the expectation of the presentation is strictly to entertain). And sometimes the communicator has a more ambitious goal: to change the audience's thinking about something in order to respond differently to a set of circumstances.

Each of these strategies will be explored in greater depth in the essays and examples to follow.

Pulpit Notes #1: **A First Communion Homily**

(Throughout the text, this book will include examples from homilies and presentations that illustrate the issues and challenges being discussed. A note about the layout of these homilies: These texts are purposely broken down into "sense lines." Each line of text concludes at a natural "break" or pause point—the end of a sentence or clause, the conclusion of an idea, a place where the speaker would naturally stop or take a break [a similar layout is used in the current Lectionary]. This layout of the text makes it much easier to "hear" the text as you are writing it and to "speak" the text when you are preaching. As you rehearse with this layout, you come to "feel" the rhythm of the piece and "hear" immediately what words need to be emphasized and grouped together. Practicing and working with text laid out this way helps you come to know the homily—and to make the words yours.)

The following two homilies respond to specific communications challenges.

This first homily was preached at a First Communion liturgy. The practice at this particular parish is having groups of eight to ten second-graders make their First Communion at one of the parish's weekend Masses. Each student is seated with his or her family, with the First Communicant seated by the aisle.

The homilist realizes the uniqueness of this audience and the circumstances. What he wants to get across to the boys and girls is that to receive this bread is to receive the very love of Jesus. So he skips the pulpit and goes down to the center aisle where the students are seated and speaks directly to them. His full attention is on the children, not the adult members of the congregation.

He begins with a story about the hat he is holding:

> I want to tell you about this cap.
> My nephew and godson Ben bought this for me
> when he was just a little older than you are.
>
> It was Christmastime,
> and this particular Christmas,
> Ben wanted not only to get presents
> but he wanted to give them, as well.
> So he saved his allowance
> and did extra work to earn money to buy presents.
>
> On Christmas morning, there was a box for me from Ben.
> And inside the box was this New England Patriots hat.
> Ben knew that I'm a big Patriots fan.
>
> I've gotten a lot of great Christmas presents in my life—
> but this cap is one of the best.
> Why? It's just a cap.
> But I know the hard work and sacrifice that went into buying this cap for me.
>
> When I wear this cap,
> most people see just a neat Patriots cap.

But for me, it's a lot more than that.
Every time I wear it,
I feel Ben's love for me
and remember all he did to get it for me.

It's the same with this piece of bread.
        [The homilist holds up an unconsecrated Communion wafer.]
To most people, it looks like just a flat, not-terribly-tasty piece of bread.
But we know it's more than that.
We know what Jesus did to give us this bread:
    how he lived for us and died for us and rose from the dead for us.
And this bread is what he gave us to remember him by.
This is how he wanted us to remember him and be a part of our lives.
And so, when Father John asks God to send his Spirit down upon this bread,
this bread *becomes* Jesus:
it *becomes* his love and care for us.
Just like that Patriots hat is, for me, the love of my nephew Ben,
this bread and wine is, for you and me, the love of Jesus.

So why should this bread matter to these kids? The homilist continues:

But the best thing of all is this:
We can become what we receive.
We can become what we receive.

You can *become* the love you receive in Holy Communion.
When you do something good for someone else,
you've become what you've received in Holy Communion.
When you help Mom and Dad,
when you're kind to your brothers and sisters,
when you give your time to someone who needs you,
when you do the best you can,
you've *become* what you've received:
you've become the love of Jesus that you've received in Holy Communion.

So this is a big day. It's a happy day.
We all hope that this First Communion is the first of many, many times
    you come to receive Jesus in Communion.

And our best wish for you is this:
>   that you may become what you receive here;
>   that you may become the love and care of Jesus himself . . .

Congratulations—and welcome to Jesus' table . . .

The homilist knows his audience. He realizes the limits of their comprehension (and attention span) and the limits of their experience. There is no talk about transubstantiation or *epiclesis* this morning. The *one* point he wants to make: in receiving this bread, we receive Jesus—and the love of Jesus that we receive we can also become.

The story about the football cap engages the second-graders because it is something they can see and understand on several levels: they have all received gifts like that themselves, and maybe they've even given gifts like that. At this stage of their young lives, they are beginning to appreciate the value and meaning of signs in their lives: things that mean more than just what they are. While the concept of the Eucharist as mystery may still be beyond their grasp, they know that this "bread" is indeed special. The homilist understands the limits of their understanding and works within those limits.

In making the connections between the Eucharist (what we receive) and the good that we do in our everyday lives (what we become), the homilist makes the homily *matter* to these children. He shows them that this altar table is an extension of their family table, that the love they receive here is part of the love they give and receive every day of their lives.

Simple, to-the-point—and sound—sacramental theology.

Pulpit Notes #2: Funeral Homily for Fred the Printer

Preaching at funerals is a challenge for every homilist. Often funeral homilies have to be written with very little lead time—and, more and more often, priests and deacons are called to preside at funerals for souls with little or no connection with the parish.

A funeral homily is not intended to serve as a eulogy. It is not a tribute or memorial to the deceased, but, like any good homily, it is the proclamation of the Word of God: the grace and hope of the resurrection that is the inheritance of all who are baptized in Christ.

That said, it is important to realize that the homily is addressed to a grieving community, a circle of family and friends who are saying good-bye to a loved one. An important part of the ministry of such a proclamation is helping this community of mourners behold the presence of God in this life that ends and begins.

The following homily was preached at the funeral for Fred, a printer respected throughout the community. The homilist is a deacon who knew Fred from his own work in publishing.

He begins by inviting family and friends to see Fred and his work in a new and different light:

> I suspect that, if he had lived a few hundred years later,
> Saint Paul would have been a printer.
> As it was, Paul was a craftsman.
> He made his living as a tentmaker.
> He was skilled in working with leather, cloth, and animal skins.
> But in one of his letters to the church he founded in Corinth,
> Paul writes this to the Christians there:
> "You are a letter of Christ,
>> a letter not written in ink but of the Spirit of God,
>> letters not etched on tablets of stone
>> but letters written on tablets of heart and flesh."
>>> *(see 2 Corinthians 3:2-3)*
>
> The perfect image for this day when we commend Fred to God.
>
> One of the best parts of the work I do has been working with printers—
> especially master printers who know what it's like to be up to their elbows
>> in gooey ink,
> printers who know the precision required to work with small pieces of lead,
> printers who know the intricate gears of a Mergenthaler press.
>
> There aren't many great printers left.
>
> Fred was a great printer.

While most congregations would not understand many of the above references, this gathering of Fred's family and friends—including other printers in the area—knows exactly what the homilist is talking about.

You always sensed that Fred not only loved what he did
but that he respected the art of printing
and that he was grateful for what he had learned and the skill he was blessed
        with.
And Fred readily gave back what he received:
Fred mentored many young journeymen printers over the years,
who came to share both his respect for the craft and the excellence it
        required.

Fred's own standards transcended whatever the spec sheet said.
Whatever his clients' expectations,
Fred, first, had to satisfy himself.
Fred was his own toughest client.
And when it came to quality, Fred took no prisoners.

Fred also understood and respected the power of letters, of words, of color,
        of images.
Stop and think for a moment about the number of people
who read something Fred printed over
his more than half-century in the business—
all the people who learned something,
whose lives were made more productive,
whose businesses prospered,
whose dreams were realized,
whose spirits were lifted and inspired,
by some piece Fred printed.
Quite a legacy, when you think about it.

But Fred's life was more than "letters of ink."
Fred was about "letters of spirit" and "words written on the heart."
His family was his joy.
He took care of everyone.
The same hard work and sense of gratitude that made Fred a great printer
made him a great husband, father, grandfather, and great-grandfather,
a great brother, cousin, and uncle,
a great colleague, neighbor, and friend.

"Letters not of ink but of spirit,
words not written on stone but on the heart."

Now the homilist comes to the point—why this particular moment *matters*:

> When our Catholic tribe gathers for the funeral of one of our own,
> the funeral celebration focuses on two themes.
>
> The first is thanksgiving.
> We come here to give *thanks*.
> The word *Eucharist*—
> > the sacrament we are about to celebrate around this table—
> > comes from the Greek word meaning *thanksgiving*.
> Every time we celebrate the Mass, the Eucharist, we are giving thanks—
> we thank God for the gift of life itself;
> we thank God for the gift of Jesus,
> > the very Word of God made human for us,
> > who shows us how to create heaven in our own place and time;
> we thank God for his Spirit of love that unites us
> > as family and friends and church
> > in compassion, forgiveness, justice, and peace.
>
> And, at this altar today, we also give thanks for the gift of Fred.
> In Fred's generosity of spirit and greatness of heart,
> > we came to know the love of God in our midst.
>
> And the second theme of our gathering this morning is *commendation*.
> At the end of this Mass, we will pray the Rite of Commendation.
> We *commend* Fred to God:
> > commend, from the Latin word *commendare*, to entrust.
> We *entrust* to God the soul of Fred, whom God lovingly takes into his care.
> We give back to God what God has given us.
> In entrusting Fred to God for eternity,
> we place our faith and trust in God's continuing circle of life:
> > God creating us and re-creating us,
> > God sustaining us and redeeming us,
> > God lifting us up when we stumble,
> > God healing us when we break,
> > God calling us back to him again and again and again.
> It is a circle formed of that mysterious, unfathomable, limitless, unconditional
> > love of God—

and in that love, we are bound to God and to one another.
We become sources of comfort and support for one another
    as we struggle to say our good-byes to Fred.

That circle of life was what Fred was all about:
complete, unconditional love.
Whenever you were in Fred's presence,
he made sure you were part of that circle—
whether you were in Fred's home, on his beloved boat, in his shop.

So, despite our grief, despite the big empty place that Fred so joyfully filled
    in our hearts,
let us give thanks to God that Fred was a part of our lives;
let us commend Fred to God with the prayer that we may embrace the spirit
    of God that drove Fred's life and work:
to become ourselves what Fred was:
    "Letters not of ink but of spirit,
    words not written on stone but on the heart."

A good funeral homily cannot be a boilerplate. Every funeral homily (and wedding homily, as well) is a unique moment in an individual's life and in the history of a family. It *matters* to them in a very intimate, loving way. The challenge for the homilist is to reveal to them the presence of God's love in that moment.

Communicaré

(Each chapter of this book will conclude with a section titled *Communicaré* [pronounced in Latin: co-mune-i-KAH-ray]. These end-of-the-chapter sections will include questions to consider as you go about the ministry of communicating the Word of God or offer practices and techniques to help improve your writing or delivery. These *Communicaré* sections will also challenge you to consider how you might deal with a particular pastoral situation that requires a more unique, "outside-the-box" strategy for articulating the Word of God. The hope is that these *Communicaré* questions may be a source of both effective strategizing and focused prayer in your ministry of proclamation.)

Take a look at this Sunday's gospel. What one single word strikes you as important on this particular day or time in your life or the life of the parish? What one sentence or description resonates with you? What does this gospel inspire you to do or respond?

How do you imagine this gospel being heard by a young parent? A teenager or college student? A First Communion class? The resident of an assisted-living facility? How would you explain your "take" on this gospel to an unbeliever? How does this gospel make you uncomfortable?

Have any radio, television, or print ads struck you of late, that "worked" on you? Where do you see each of the four strategies discussed in this chapter: *focusing on one central idea, engaging your interest, winning your trust, compelling you to act?*

CHAPTER 2

The Sunday "Conversation"

A single mother wakes up one morning thinking only about how much work she has to accomplish at the office. But before she even gets dressed, her seven-year-old son begins to complain about a sore throat. She begins her first argument of the day by asking him, "Just how sore is it, really?" After his continued protests, she checks in his mouth and realizes he's not going to be able to go to school. So she quickly burns through her entire list of babysitters before finally talking someone into watching him. By then, she's late for her first appointment at the office, which leads to a scolding from her boss. That leaves her grumpy enough to start an argument with her secretary, who had nothing to do with the boy's sore throat. It isn't even ten a.m., and her whole day is already consumed by an irrational chaos of successive arguments, which are really all variations on her basic struggle to make the day work out well.

Should this woman stumble into church after a week of this frustration, she is not going to be accustomed to hearing that there is any sacred mystery to her life. She may be hoping that her pastor will provide more tips or strategies for holding together the competing demands on her life. Worse yet, she may come to church seeking only some spiritual entertainment that will distract her from the insanity of her week. But what she really needs is a vision of the holiness of her life, as uncontrollable as it will always be.

—M. Craig Barnes, *The Pastor as Minor Poet* [1]

And so begins the Sunday "conversation," that conversation the homilist invites this mom to be a part of.

Where is the "holy" in our lives? How do we experience the sacred in the course of our very ordinary days? Where is God in this chaos that is our lives?

Many preachers are quite adept at pointing out where God is *not*. But most of us know all too well where Sodom and Gomorrah intersect in our lives; we are painfully aware of the failures, the broken pieces and, yes, the sin in our lives.

The challenge each Sunday is to tell us where God *is* in our lives, to make the connections between the reality of the community's life and the hope of the Gospel.

Consider for a moment why our Christian forebears called this a "homily." The word *homily* is derived from the Greek word for "conversation." The first Christian communities used the word *homilia* to describe this reflection by the presider. They did not see this particular moment in the Eucharist as a formal proclamation of the Word of God (*kerygma*) or as an explanation of the practices and rituals that derive from the Word (*didache*) or as a detailed analysis of the major ethical and moral issues of the day in light of the Word (*parenesis*). They saw the speaker's purpose here as applying the Word to the daily life of the speaker's hearers. This particular moment was about the struggle to love as God has loved us, about living Jesus' Word in our everyday struggles in trying to provide for our families, about discovering God in the messiness of our lives.

Perspective, Tone, Language

The Sunday conversation that is the homily is about letting the busy single mom know that, despite the complexities and demands of her days, her life is indeed holy.

If this communication is *homilia*, a conversation, it has implications for the participants—and please note the plural.

First, a conversation is *an exchange between equals*. A superior and his or her underling do not stand on the same level—any real exchange of ideas between the two is difficult and unlikely. The perspective of the superior on the higher step typically prevails over those who are answerable to him or her. In most of these exchanges, the superior has decided on a course of action; the communication between both parties is about how and when to carry it out.

But a conversation takes place between and among "equals." *Homilia* is centered on the common experience of the participants, friends who share memories and experiences, fellow pilgrims who assist each other along the road they all travel.

Granted, in the preaching dynamic, there is only one party doing the actual "talking." But those who are "only" listening are still engaged in the "conversation." They respond by their eye contact, facial expressions, and body movement. They also possess the power to tune out the speaker altogether. In addition, members of the community may also participate in the conversation by offering their observations and criticisms to the homilist after Mass (if the homilist is perceived by the community to be approachable and open).

But, most important, their participation in the "conversation" is determined by the degree to which they recognize themselves and their lives in the homily; they will be engaged in this exchange to the extent that this homily *matters* to them.

The *tone* of the homily reflects that commonality, that equality of all before God. The homily should invite, inspire, and welcome. It engages the community by drawing from the experiences and challenges we all face.

The tone is centered on humility. Gospel-centered humility is not diminishing oneself or, at its worst, self-abnegation or humiliation. Humility is the realization that every one of us is a child of God, that every one of us stands before God as equals, that every human being possesses the sacred dignity of being created in the image and likeness of God. Humility is to realize that the hopes and dreams of that single mom in the eighth pew are just as important and valid as those of the CEO in the fourth pew; humility is to recognize that she is as loved by God in her everyday struggles as is the celebrant of this liturgy. The faithful homilist approaches the ambo with such humility: the humility of a God who "emptied" himself of his divinity to become human so that humanity might realize its own sacred dignity. Such a spirit of humility strikes the "right" tone of love and respect for one's brother and sister travelers.

Most of us would have no trouble coming up with an endless list of evil and sin plaguing our world. Evil we understand and recognize. True, we may not readily acknowledge it in ourselves, but we immediately see it and experience it around us. More often than not, we have come to accept evil as just the way things are. Ethical shortcuts and moral trade-offs are the costs of doing business. Self-centeredness has become the norm.

And certainly such a view of sin should be addressed. Sin is a reality for all of us—not just for "them" and certainly not just for "you." Sin is a reality for all of us—homilist included.

But pointing to human failure and sinfulness is easy. The real challenge of preaching is to point to the holiness in our lives in images that we can see and feel, in language that is affecting and real, not pietistic or banal. The single mom, overwhelmed with the demands on her as a parent and professional, is well aware that her life is less than ideal, that God is at the edges of her life, if at all. The homilist's work is to show her that God is at the center of her life. The Sunday conversation should help her realize that her love for her child is sacred, that God is a reality in her day-to-day decision-making, that the love of God is as present in her home and around her table as it is at the altar in her church.

The Sunday "conversation" is also distinguished by its *language*. This is not a theological discourse. Though centered in Scripture, it is not intended to be a detailed exegesis of the text. The homiletic moment is not "the deacon's time" to rail and rant on whatever moves him.

The homily is about *us*, all of us. And so it has to be spoken in a language we all can understand, in words that mean something to us. It has to be spoken in words that are clear and can be grasped in their first hearing (remember: the homily is *heard* by the community, not read).

Every organization has its own jargon, its own set of words and symbols that have a particular meaning for those who belong to the group. Jargon is an organization's "shorthand." And our Catholic tribe has its own verbal "shorthand," to be sure. And within the church, different communities and constituencies have their own codes: liturgical language, scriptural language, canonical language. Presuming that the Sunday community understands the words and concepts as the homilist means them and understands them can lead to a disconnect in the conversation.

Jesuit Father Thomas Reese writes about his own experience preaching: "As a young priest, I did make a promise to myself that I would never use words in a homily that did not make sense to me. As a result, I usually avoid phrases like 'saving souls,' 'God's grace' and 'transubstantiation' because I am not sure what those words mean. They are abstractions that don't touch me. On the other hand, love, compassion and mercy are words that I can connect with."[2]

What exactly is "grace"—and how do I "get" it?

How do I experience "salvation" in my life?

Why should I care about "transubstantiation"?

Such words and phrases raise more questions than many preachers realize.

The Sunday homily should be spoken in the language of the everyday. Just as Jesus preached in parables about lost sheep, wayward children, and planting seeds, preachers today connect with their hearers most effectively in stories of the holy and sacred in their communities: stories and images about juggling school and sports schedules, about making one's way through the many moral quagmires of making a living, about ethical dilemmas that were unimaginable just a generation ago.

The homilist cannot stand back and pretend to be a detached observer of life. He or she is a full participant in all of life's joys and sorrows, a life that the preacher shares with every member of the congregation. The Word proclaimed cannot stand apart and aloof from the landscape but be grounded in the very midst of it.

Effective preaching, therefore, is *incarnational*. God's becoming human did not end with the physical life of Jesus. God continues to be experienced in the physical and the human realities of love, of hurt, of discovery, of suffering. The Sunday conversation is about finding God in life—life in all its messiness and ugliness, life in all its struggles and confusions, life in all its failures and disappointments. The Sunday sermon/homily has to be grounded in the Monday-through-Saturday life of the community. It must point to the presence of God in the midst of our "ploughing" and planting, our laughing and crying, our headaches and heartthrobs. As Christ reveals to us a God who is the loving Father of his children, the preacher is called to reveal that same God who comforts, consoles, illuminates, and animates our lives.

"Authentic" Preaching

Every effective communication is centered in the audience. The world of advertising is littered with campaigns that failed because the message was more about the sender than the receiver.

Like any ministry, the homily is at the service of the community. It requires the same spirit of the Jesus who washed the feet of his disciples in the Cenacle on Holy Thursday night. The homilist must put aside his or her own "cloak" of expectations and certainties and bend down and deal with the everyday dust and dirt that collects on his hearers. The homily that ministers is spoken in the language of the community; it employs stories and images that are real and authentic to its hearers; it confronts the questions that those who gather are asking. The homilist/footwasher puts aside his or her own agenda and perspective and the comfort of personal spirituality in order to pick up the towel and plunge his or her hands into the water of the basin.

Not that the homilist should not challenge the community—but the homilist always understands where the community is at that moment regarding this particular issue, why they feel as they do (whether positively or negatively), and leads them from there. The homilist invites (not demands) a new, Christ-centered way of looking at a question or issue.

The Millennial generation is presenting a particular challenge in the Sunday conversation. Every demographic and sociological profile of the Millennials—the 80 million strong, born between 1980 and 2000—shows a generation that is pragmatic and realistic, neither dreamers nor romantics. Self-centered? Some. But what drives them is a sense of purpose—they want their lives to *mean* something. They don't care about establishments and institutions; they're more interested in relationships (family and friends). They are not joiners. They are not impressed by power. They want to *do* meaningful and important things.

Time magazine reporter Joel Stein writes in his May 2013 cover story on the Millennials, "They're not into going to church, even though they believe in God, because they don't identify with big institutions; one-third of adults under 20, the highest percentage ever, are religiously unaffiliated. They want new experiences, which are more important to them than material goods."[3]

Rachel Held Evans writes of her generation's search for meaning and its tenuous relationship with the institutional church. What young would-be Christians seek is *authenticity*:

> If young people are looking for congregations that authentically practice the teachings of Jesus in an open and inclusive way, then

the good news is the church already knows how to do that. The trick isn't to make church cool; it's to keep worship weird.

You can get a cup of coffee with your friends anywhere, but church is the only place you can get ashes smudged on your forehead as a reminder of your mortality. You can be dazzled by a light show at a concert on any given weekend, but church is the only place that fills a sanctuary with candlelight and hymns on Christmas Eve. . . . You can share food with the hungry at any homeless shelter, but only the church teaches that a shared meal brings us into the very presence of God.

Evans remembers her own return to church as a young adult:

What finally brought me back, after years of running away, wasn't lattes or skinny jeans; it was the sacraments. Baptism, confession, Communion, preaching the Word, anointing the sick—you know, those strange rituals and traditions Christians have been practicing for the past 2,000 years. The sacraments are what make the church relevant, no matter the culture or era. They don't need to be repackaged or re-branded; they just need to be practiced, offered and explained in the context of a loving, authentic and inclusive community.[4]

That's the present and future challenge to pastors and preachers: to make the church a place where communicants can do good and meaningful things, where they can love others, where they can experience God in relationship and community. The community seeks homilies that reveal the love of God in the midst of the good we do and are: God in our families, God in our work, God in our school, God among our friends, God in our community.

The homily is subject to the same tensions and challenges as any form of communication. An engaging conversation does that: in the midst of such divisions and anxieties, it finds points of connection and binds the participants in a common understanding, a shared vision, a resolve to act for the good of all.

But listeners approach the homily as they do any message they come in contact with—from a podcast to a television commercial—with one set of questions: *What's in this for me? Why should I engage in this conversation? Why should I do what this person (whether advertiser, candidate, beggar, or homilist) is asking me to do? How will my life be better if I respond as I'm being asked?*

Precious few homilists answer those questions on Sunday. And the result is boredom on the part of the community. The essence of boredom is noninvolvement—the "bored" congregation is not tuning out because they are not entertained but because they are not engaged in what the homilist is saying; they are bored with church not because it's not fun but because the liturgical experience is not opening their hearts and spirits to the presence of God. A conversation that must be *endured* does not engage.

"Boring" homilies fail to connect the gospel with the lived reality of the community. A "bored" listener has decided that this homily is not about him or her. The tone, the language, the perspective of the homilist, and his or her message do not connect with a bored community. But a homily that engages the community enables that community to see themselves in the mirror of the gospel. They recognize themselves in this encounter with Jesus and realize the love of God in their midst.

So begin by understanding why this is called a *homily*. It's not a lecture by an all-knowing sage; it's not the orders of the week from the home office; it's not a reprimand by a superior; it's not the personal soapbox of the guy in charge. It's a *conversation* (presented, admittedly, in a heightened, more formal rhetorical format) between and among fellow pilgrims, brother and sister disciples, engaged in the same struggle to find God in their lives and to realize the kingdom of God in their time and place.

Pulpit Notes: Tables

The following homily was preached on the evangelist John's account of Jesus feeding the multitude with a few pieces of bread and fish (John 6:1-15, the gospel reading for the Seventeenth Sunday in Ordinary Time B).

The story of Jesus' feeding of the crowds is the only miracle of Jesus that is recorded in all four gospels. What distinguishes John's version of the story is the little boy who offers Jesus his lunch that begins the miracle.

What does this miracle story say to the folks gathered in this place on this Sunday morning? The homilist begins in a place we all know, but makes his hearers see it in a new light:

Consider, for a moment, the holiest place in your home—
the place where everyone's busy lives intersect,
where all of our busy schedules come together.
It's a place we largely take for granted:
the family table.

Yeah, that table—in all its chipped, Crayola-marked, scratched glory—
the first landing place for backpacks, keys, the mail, and unfolded laundry;
the table that sometimes serves as a homework desk,
sometimes your office,
sometimes a workbench,
sometimes a confessional,
and, every once in a while, we even manage to have a meal together at it.
It is the one place where we are family together.
Around the family table, we experience God's greatest blessings:
the very gift of our lives and the gifts of the earth to sustain them.

And, because of that, your table is a holy place—
God is as present at your family table as he is in any church or shrine.

The family table is a level playing field:
everyone matters there,
everyone's joys are celebrated there,
everyone's problems and hurts are taken on there
    by the other members of the family.

At our family table, we are always welcomed,
no matter what we have done or how the other members of the family may
        feel about us on a given day.

The family table is the place where decisions are made,
problems are confronted if not resolved,
lessons are learned.

At the family table, we hear the stories about our families—
we learn where we came from, we discover who we are.
To be welcomed to another family's dinner table is a special invitation
that is not extended to everyone—
we'll go out to a restaurant with "associates,"

but we invite to our family's table only our best and most cherished friends
—those we love like "family."

Your family table—whether located in a formal dining room or a cluttered kitchen—
is more than just a piece of furniture.
It's the place where God makes his presence known in your midst:
in bread shared,
in the unspoken but understood welcome to all who have a place around it,
in the healing and support and forgiveness found there.

Your family table is a holy place,
your family table is a *sacramental* place . . .

Note the language here. It's not scholarly or pietistic. It's simple and
real. The language is also highly descriptive: the homilist is describing
real tables here, not some highly stylized, perfect, Martha Stewart-
designed dining room. Listeners can "see" their table and their families
gathered around it.
    From that image, the homilist offers a new vision of their tables:

Our life as a church community is centered on sacraments.
At our parish table, we gather to celebrate the "capital S" Sacraments
in which we meet the risen Christ in our midst,
in which we realize our call to be his church in our time and place,
in which we support one another in the work of discipleship,
in which our lives mesh with Christ's.
We all pretty much get that . . .

But our lives are filled with "small s" sacraments, as well,
in which we encounter God in the "stuff" of our everyday lives:
the "small s" sacraments we "celebrate"
in which we discover the love and mercy of God within our own families,
        in our classrooms and workplaces.

In today's gospel reading,
we heard the story of Jesus feeding the crowd.
The feeding of the multitude is the only miracle of Jesus'
that is recorded in all four gospels.
The story must have been cherished by the first Christian communities.

The story is the same in all four gospels:
It's been a long day; people are hungry;
Jesus takes a few scraps of bread and pieces of fish,
gives thanks for them, blesses them,
and breaks them to give to the hungry crowd.

But in John's version the story includes one detail the other three versions
     don't:
the little boy.
In John's story, it's a little boy who gives his lunch to Jesus.
The pieces of bread and fish are the boy's.
Jesus' miracle begins with the boy's generosity.
Jesus' "capital S" Sacrament is possible because of the boy's "small s"
     sacrament.

A boy's lunch, generously offered, is the making of a miracle.
And that is sacrament.

Today, consider all the "small s" sacraments that you celebrate, that you make
     possible:
the supper you prepare each night with and for your family . . .
the time you make to listen to a friend whose life has taken a nightmarish
     turn . . .
the unexpected card of congratulations or sympathy or support . . .

We are a sacramental church:
We see the good we do and the blessings we receive as sacrament—
the manifestation of God's love present in our lives.
We behold the presence of God in the everyday joys and blessings, the
     struggles and messes of life.
Our "capital S" sacraments in which we celebrate the risen Christ in our
     midst
continue in our "small s" sacraments of kindness and mercy and generosity
     and forgiveness.
And your family table is a place where many of those sacraments begin . . .

Though "formally" delivered by the homilist from the ambo, the dynamics of this piece are conversational: it's about *us* (not *you*, not *I*). It centers on an image from the everyday world of the community (the table). It is articulated in the language of the listeners ("small s" sacraments) rather than the heady language of canons and doctrines. And all the pieces come together to engage the community in realizing the love of God in their midst.

The single mom raising her precious little boy, who has had another overwhelmingly demanding week, finds peace in seeing a little more clearly God's presence in the middle of it all.

Communicaré

Think about the community at Mass last weekend. Imagine individual faces you saw as you preached. What do you think each of those folks took from the homily last Sunday?

Look at the texts of your last two or three homilies. Are there words and phrases that you use often? Are there words and phrases you use that you presume your community understands, but may not? For each of these words and phrases you use frequently, write out in a hundred words or less what you mean by them: words and phrases like *grace, compassion, justice, salvation, mercy, sacrament.*

Underline in the text of your recent homilies words and images that your listeners can readily see in their lives. Cross out words or phrases that are merely concepts and ideas that remain unexplained or undeveloped, that you never "show" your listeners.

Read this Sunday's gospel. Can you remember a time or place or situation in your life in which you experienced this gospel story?

CHAPTER 3

Four Questions

Writing and delivering an effective homily each week begins with what the late Father Walter Burghardt called "mulling" over the Sunday gospel: spending time (ideally several days) praying with and over the text, letting the words simmer in the preacher's mind and heart, playing with the images, understanding what this gospel might have to say to a community living the paschal mystery today—until a promising central idea bursts forth.[1]

To really "mull" over the text can't be done with a deadline looming—"mulling" demands more time than Saturday morning, just hours before the liturgy. Practically speaking, the "mulling" process should begin at least a week before you preach, with a prayerful (out loud) reading of the following week's gospel, then a rereading of the text the following morning and again in the evening and then every morning and evening, letting the Word of God percolate in your consciousness as you go about the week.

(One of the great advantages that many deacons have here is that they don't preach every week; therefore, they can—and should—spend a week or more "mulling" over the gospel before beginning the work of writing the homily.)

Such "mulling" is a form of prayer, prayer in which you listen to God speaking in this text—but this "mulling" process is not confined to sitting in church with the lectionary on your lap. In this praying/mulling process, the gospel becomes a lens through which you see your world. More often than not, you will "see" this gospel come alive in a conversation with someone, in something you see or hear or read, in a decision you have to make. Don't try to write your homily or "find" the hook for your homily just yet. Just go through your days, carry on your work and meetings.

And "mull."

(An important note: If you are new to the ministry of preaching the Sunday gospel, your principal "textbook" is the Sunday Lectionary, the collection of readings assigned to each Sunday and solemnity of the liturgical year. There is a method and pattern to the design and order of the readings. If you have not done so, read the Introduction to the Lectionary, especially chapters 4 and 5, which explain how the readings are ordered according to season and how a Sunday's assigned gospel, readings, and responsorial psalm all relate to one another. The essays in this book focus on the gospel as the centerpiece, the "high point" of the Liturgy of the Word, as the introduction says in paragraph 13. As such, the day's assigned gospel reading—in Greek, *pericope*—should be the focus of the homily.)

The "mulling" stage is not about figuring out what you're going to say but discovering what Christ is teaching, revealing, and doing in this particular text. Your "mulling" might center around four questions.

What Is the Single Most Striking Word, Sentence, or Image in This Gospel?

There are images and phrases in the gospel that are especially striking: the "good" shepherd; "it cannot be that way with you"; the father who begs Jesus to heal his daughter; "fear is useless"; the grain of wheat that dies to realize its harvest. What single word or image or sentence in this pericope strikes you? Over time, you will be amazed at what words and pictures capture your imagination.

For example, in Jesus' encounter with the tax collector Zacchaeus, who climbs a tree in order to see Jesus above the crowds (Luke 19:1-10), Jesus calls out to him, "Zacchaeus, come down quickly, for today I must stay at your house." Zacchaeus, who is distrusted if not despised by his neighbors because of his profession, comes down from the tree and welcomes Jesus, despite the grumbling of onlookers. After inviting himself to dinner, Jesus assures Zacchaeus, "Today salvation has come to this house . . ."

Mull over that sentence: "Today salvation has come to this house." What does such "salvation" look like? How do we experience "salvation" in our houses?

In the course of mulling/praying over that word, one homilist realized the many times that parents experience Jesus' "salvation." He and his wife and their friends who were moms and dads all had experiences similar to this:

> Teenage daughter had been in a foul mood
> for what seemed like an eternity.
> When her wise and patient mother had had enough of the sulking and
>   eye-rolling,
> she sent the rest of the family off to the movies.
> Loading up with her daughter's favorite ice cream,
> Mom called her into the kitchen and told her to have a seat.
> Mom scooped two big bowls.
> Nothing was said for a long time.
> But by the second and third scoops, the teenager began to open up.
> Mother and daughter talked the afternoon away.
> Because of a mother's patience, love—
>   and a couple of pints of Ben & Jerry's—
> *salvation comes to this house.*

As the gospel story "percolated" in his consciousness over a few days, the homilist began to see how, in our own humble efforts at kindness and understanding and our seemingly inconsequential acts of generosity and forgiveness, we can bring to our own homes the salvation that Jesus brings to the house of the faithful Zacchaeus in this gospel.

Throughout the gospels, Jesus drives out "demons" from those who are "possessed." Our understanding of mental illness has progressed light years from the time of Jesus, but the idea of "demons" and "possession" captured the imagination of one homilist. Preparing to preach on Jesus' curing of the possessed man at the synagogue in Capernaum (Mark 1:21-28), the homilist began to think about how individuals can be "possessed" by "demons." Several examples came to light in the course of his "mulling":

> Forty-five years ago,
> he was nineteen years old and walking a patrol in the jungles of Vietnam.
> The nightmares continue to this day:
> buddies dying suddenly and instantly at his side,
> innocent children burned and mutilated,
> the stinging napalm burning his eyes and nostrils.

He's tried everything—drugs, alcohol, therapy—
but he can't escape the memories and the images etched in his mind.
He is a prisoner of the *demons* of war . . .

She is in her late thirties.
She spends her days stocking shelves and ringing up sales.
She makes a few cents more than minimum wage.
And each night she returns to her small, empty apartment.
Just a year ago she was happily married—or so she thought.
But her life and marriage came crashing down in betrayal and acrimony.
Now she is alone and terrified at the prospect of meeting anyone and
      engaging in any kind of relationship.
Her greatest fear is being hurt again.
She is "possessed" by the *demons* of fear and brokenness . . .

He flunked out.
He didn't know how to handle the new responsibilities of being on his own.
Without someone like Mom or Dad or his coach or counselor pushing him,
he couldn't manage the demands of his studies and work schedule.
He had worked hard to get into this first-tier university—
but the immensity of the school swallowed him up.
He's home now,
working dead-end part-time jobs that he thought he had left behind forever
      when he graduated from high school.
His parents are understanding and supportive—
but he knows they are disappointed
and he realizes the major outlay of tuition that was lost in his failed freshman
      year.
He has no idea what to do next.
He is swallowed up by the *demons* of failure . . .

In his prayer/mulling over the story of Jesus curing the man possessed, the homilist came to recognize the "demons" that exist in all
our lives. Traumatic experiences, emotional disasters, and shattered
dreams trap us, enslave us, cripple us; these "demons" so drain us of
hope that we surrender to them rather than confront them. Such heal-
ings are central to Jesus' revelation of the reign of God: God's dream
that no one be imprisoned or enslaved by the tragedies of life or be left
to stumble and fall alone in the darkness. And now Jesus calls all of

us to the work of driving out those "demons" that divide our families, sever friendships, and rend our spirits in hopelessness and despair by the power of our own compassion, forgiveness, and understanding.

So what word or phrase strikes you in this gospel reading? One of the wonders of Scripture is that one word or phrase or image may strike you today, while next week or month or year you may find an entirely different image from the reading compelling. Take your thinking where the Spirit leads you on this given day. And don't worry that you'll run out of surprises in a gospel pericope—you will always find a new idea to mine in Jesus' gospel.

You might consider, too, how a gospel text would read if Jesus were speaking today. What images would Jesus use today if he were preaching this gospel? For example, how would he cast the parable of the Good Samaritan in this parish? Or what images would Jesus use to preach the Beatitudes in twenty-first-century America? What would the rich young man or woman we know respond to Jesus' imperative that they sell all they have for the sake of the poor?

Reconsider the details of the story. Recast the characters and situations. Imagine this gospel playing out in your home, in your community, in your parish.

Where and How Do We See This Gospel in Our Time and Place?

Look around. Who in your parish is the generous widow, the prodigal's father, the woman seeking justice, the father begging for his son's cure?

Who are the saints in your life: the Elizabeths and Zechariahs, the Annas and Simeons, the Mary Magdalenes, the Zacchaeuses, the faithful and compassionate myrrh bearers of Easter morning?

When have you heard God calling you as he calls to Mary in the appearance of Gabriel? When have you been confronted with the need to forgive and heal as the prodigal's father must do for the sake of his family? How have you experienced the generosity of the widow who readily gives her entire livelihood of a few pennies or been challenged by the dubious promise of the mustard seed?

What exactly is going on in this particular gospel? Go deeper into the text. Why does Jesus say what he does? What are the cultural, political, and psychological factors involved here? When Jesus speaks about marriage, for example, what is the cultural understanding of marriage that Jesus is confronting? Why are palm branches waved by the crowds as

Jesus enters Jerusalem? What makes the Pharisees tick? Why were tax collectors so detested? What was life like for a shepherd?

Consider, for example, the story of Gabriel's announcing to Mary that she is to be the mother of the Christ (Luke 1:26-38). Do we experience such annunciations in our lives? When and how does God call you to "give birth" to Christ in the Nazareth of your parish, the Bethlehem of your home?

In an essay in *The Christian Century*, Lauren F. Winner "mulls" over the story of the annunciation (Luke 1:26-38). Winner, assistant professor of Christian Spirituality at Duke Divinity School, wonders how she would have responded to God's "interruption" of her life:

> I have often wondered what I would have said in Mary's shoes. Would I have said "Fiat mihi"? I doubt it. I think I would probably say, "Excuse me?" or "Um, thank you, but I'd really rather not." The fact is, I'm not especially interested in being interrupted by God. God's plans seem rarely to coincide with my own. . . .
>
> Actually, I'm better at grand, earthquake interruptions—dramatic interruptions that require moving, changing jobs, radically redirecting life plans. . . . It's the smaller interruptions—say, the knock of an unannounced visitor on my office door—that really irk me. When I hear that unexpected knock, I turn my face into a smile and try not to communicate to my visitors that I was in the middle of a really crucial sentence and would they please leave and close the door behind them?

But in her many roles as a teacher and counselor, a spouse and ordained minister, Winner has discovered that those many interruptions may well be God knocking:

> [Such interruptions] show me to be a prideful control freak who dares to think that whatever I've got on tap for the day is supremely important and who dares to think that I own my own precious time. They are interruptions that, when I let them, foster a little humility. And it is that hard-to-swallow fruit of humility that allows me to sometimes recognize these interruptions as God's way of gradually schooling me in the grand imperatives of letting go of all I cling to and following Christ.[2]

Lauren Winner begins to see Luke's story in a new light: that our lives are a series of "interruptions" by God—"annunciations," if you will—

in which God focuses our attention on his love and mercy, his compassion and grace, in the midst of our busy lives.

Reflecting on Jesus' parable of the persistent widow (Luke 18:1-8), a homilist realized that he has met the widow in his own family and parish:

> It may be a spouse's Parkinson's disease, a parent's Alzheimer's,
>   a sister's breast cancer, a child's leukemia.
> The illness of a loved one,
> a catastrophe striking their family,
> the suffering of someone dear to them
> transforms these moms and dads and sons and daughters and friends
> into dedicated advocates and resolute guardians.
>
> They fight hospitals and insurance companies
> for the critical medical care needed by their loved one.
> They take on school systems and governments
> for the assistance and services their child is entitled to.
> They work tirelessly to raise awareness, raise money,
>   and, when necessary, raise Cain.
>
> These dedicated men and women are the gospel widow in our midst.
> They face down the "dishonest judges" of arrogance and avarice;
> they take on the "judges" of insensitivity and unawareness;
> they go toe-to-toe with the "judges who fear neither God
> nor respect any human being"—save themselves.
> Their love for the sick and suffering enables them to carry on "day and night";
> their faith and conviction in the rightness of their cause empowers them
> to carry on despite the frustration and inaction they face.
> The very compassion of God is their hope and assurance that their prayer
>   will be heard.

The persistent widow of Luke's gospel, the homilist continued, lives among us: She is the poor, the struggling, the ignored, the forgotten; she is the mother and father, the daughter and son, the family and friend of the suffering and dying who works for a cure so that other families may be spared what she has suffered through; she is the victim of injustice whose sense of her own dignity enables her to fight on. Christ promises that the Father hears the prayer of the gospel widow in her many guises, the homilist concluded, and that her perseverance in faith will one day be rewarded. And further, he offers, Jesus confronts us with our own culpability for the widow's plight when we become, in our obliviousness and self-absorption, "judges who neither fear God nor respect any human being."

In your "mulling" over Sunday's gospel, look around for the shaker of salt and the bridesmaids' oil stocks for their lamps, the blind man bold enough to ask Jesus "to see," and the farmworkers at odds with their employer. Let the gospel you are mulling/praying over serve as a lens enabling you to see the same people and things that Jesus encounters in your parish and community.

What Is Jesus Asking Us to Do?

The gospel is not a warm, fluffy blanket of charming stories. It's a call to establish God's kingdom in our time and place—but by way of the cross. God's kingdom of peace and hope is built only through sacrifice, selflessness, and generosity.

So what is Jesus asking us to do in this Sunday's gospel? And be as specific as you can. How do we respond to the situation confronted by the Good Samaritan? What are the implications of Jesus' cleansing of the temple for us in our own parish? How do we embrace the grace of the prodigal son's father when our sympathies lie with the prodigal's older brother?

Jesus' farewell discourse at the Last Supper (John 14–17) is read on the Sundays of the Easter season. In John 15:5, Jesus tells his disciples in the Cenacle, "I am the vine, you are the branches." What is the implication of that image for us as disciples, as a community of faith? What is Jesus proposing here by calling us "branches" of his "vine"? Writer Anne Lamott has experienced this "branch/vine" relationship in her own small San Francisco church. In her best-selling book *Traveling Mercies: Some Thoughts on Faith*, she writes that her son Sam is the only kid he knows who goes to church every Sunday. Lamott explains why she insists that her poor little Presbyterian church be part of her Sam's life:

> I want to give him what I found in the world, . . . a path and a little light to see by. Most of the people I know who have what I want—which is to say, purpose, heart, balance, gratitude, joy—are people with a deep sense of spirituality. They are people in community, who

pray, or practice their faith. . . . They follow a brighter light than the glimmer of their own candle. . . .

When I was at the end of my rope, the people of St. Andrew tied a knot in it for me and helped me hold on. The church became my home in the old meaning of *home*—that it's where, when you show up, they have to let you in. They let me in. They even said, "You come back now."

Sam was welcomed and prayed for at St. Andrew seven months before he was born. When I announced during worship that I was pregnant, people cheered. All these old people, raised in Bible-thumping homes in the Deep South, clapped. Even the women whose grown-up boys had been or were doing time in jails or prisons rejoiced for me. And then almost immediately they set about providing for us. They brought clothes, they brought me casseroles to keep in the freezer, they brought me assurance that this baby was going to be a part of the family. And they began slipping me money.

Now, a number of the older black women live pretty close to the bone financially on small Social Security checks. But routinely they sidled up to me and stuffed bills in my pockets—tens and twenties. . . .

I was usually filled with a sense of something like shame until I'd remember that wonderful line of Blake's—that we are here to learn to endure the beams of love—and I would take a long deep breath and force these words out of my strangulated throat: "Thank you."[3]

Anne Lamott and her congregation understand what Jesus is asking in this Easter gospel: as branches of Christ the vine, we are part of something greater than ourselves, something that transforms and transcends the fragility of our lives. So how can your family, community, and parish become extended branches for all of us who struggle to realize our own harvests of joy and discovery, of grace and faithfulness?

Jesus' parable of the wheat and weeds growing up in the same field (Matt 13:24-43) too often gets a cursory treatment by preachers: live and let live, and God will sort it out in the end. But the following story by blogger Glennon Doyle Melton, discovered by a homilist "mulling" over the text, brings a deeper understanding and contemporary insight on the parable:

Every Friday afternoon a very wise teacher asks her fifth-grade class to take out a piece of paper and write down the names of four children they would like to sit with the following week. The children all know that these requests may or may not be honored. She also asks the children to nominate one student who they believed had been an "exceptional classroom citizen" that week.

All ballots are submitted to her privately.

And every Friday, after the students leave for the weekend, she takes out the slips of paper, places them in front of her, and studies them. She looks for patterns: Who is not getting requested by anyone else? Who can't think of anyone to request? Who never gets noticed enough to be nominated? Who had a million friends last week and none this week?

The teacher is not looking for a new seating chart or "exceptional citizens." She's looking for lonely children, for children who are struggling to connect with other children, for the little ones who are falling through the cracks of the class's social life. She is discovering whose gifts are going unnoticed by their peers. And she is pinning down—immediately—who is being bullied and who is doing the bullying.

Her Friday lists are an X-ray of her classroom to see beneath the surface of things and into the hearts of her students.

She started doing this every week since the shootings at Columbine. Every single Friday since Columbine she looks at this "picture" of the students entrusted to her—because she understands that all violence begins with disconnection, that all outward violence is rooted in inner loneliness.

Being a math teacher, she understands that everything—even love, even belonging—has a pattern to it. She finds the patterns in her Friday surveys and, through those lists, she breaks the codes of disconnection. Then she gets the lonely kids the help they need.[4]

As the homilist went on to note, we tend to see people as either "good" or "bad" and take it upon ourselves to "separate" and pull up the "weeds" from our lives. But this gifted fifth-grade teacher understands that only God can separate the good from the bad—and that everyone is both "wheat" and "weed." She seeks instead to bring out and nurture the "good" that she knows exists in every one of her students.

The homilist explained that discipleship recognizes that we all possess the ability to do compassionate and good things out of love and, at the same time, there exists within us that impulse to let selfishness and fear take control of our actions and thought processes. The chal-

lenge of the parable is to possess the wisdom and generosity of heart
to harvest the "wheat" that grows in our midst despite the "weeds"
that sometimes choke us all.

How Does This Gospel Reveal God's Love in Our Midst?

Every line of the gospel challenges us—but it also assures us that
the grace of God is ours, that the love of God is constant despite our
failure to embrace it or our obtuseness to recognize it. How does the
gospel you are "mulling" over reveal that reality?

The 2013 film *Philomena* tells the true story of Philomena Lee. As
an unmarried teenager in Ireland, Philomena became pregnant and
was sent to a convent, where she had her child, a boy. As was the case
for so many poor, young, unmarried mothers in Ireland in the 1950s,
Philomena's life was a miserable existence of working in the convent
laundry, with only a few moments each day with her son. Then, one
day, without warning, the sisters handed over the little boy to an
American couple to adopt while Philomena was toiling in the laundry.
Young Philomena was devastated.

Fifty years later, Philomena enlists the help of journalist Martin
Sixsmith to help her find her son. The two could not be more contrast-
ing personalities: Philomena is openhearted and friendly, finding de-
light in the simplest things and grateful for even the smallest kindness
extended to her. The world-weary Martin is smug, sarcastic, and con-
descending. Philomena possesses great empathy and compassion; her
faith in God remains unshakable despite the hardships she has endured. Martin is trying to pick up the pieces of his once promising
journalism career that was shattered by a disastrous turn as a political
advisor; any belief he had in God died a long time ago. But the two
develop a warm respect and fondness for each other.

Philomena and Martin eventually learn what happened to
Philomena's little boy. They also realize that the nuns had deceived
and misled them every step of the way in order to cover up their
culpability. Martin is enraged and vows to expose the sisters. But
Philomena finds comfort in the fact that she now knows that her son
lived a happy, fulfilling life. She is even able to forgive the hard-hearted
Sister Hildegard, whose cruel haughtiness has not mellowed in old age.

Martin cannot understand how Philomena can be so gracious. He is
angry enough for both of them. But Philomena responds, "And what
has all your anger accomplished?" [5] Oh, it has been very hard for her,

Philomena assures Martin, but her faith in God and the good people she has come to know have brought her peace.

The grace of God is found in the Philomenas in our midst, whose own struggles and hurts enable them to understand and heal the brokenness of others. Such a vision of faith enables us to re-create our world, to shatter the darkness of injustice and hatred with the light of God's justice and compassion.

God makes himself known in the extraordinary compassion of ordinary people like Philomena Lee—and the congregation of Emanuel African Methodist Episcopal Church in Charleston, South Carolina, the scene of a horrific shooting in 2015. Most of us can't imagine something like that happening in our own church—and we're at an even greater loss wondering how we would respond to such horror. We can only pray that we would possess the faith and grace of Emanuel, in the way they loved, mourned, and graciously forgave the man accused of killing nine members of their parish, including their beloved pastor. The twenty-one-year-old shooter wandered into the group's Bible study that Wednesday evening in June and he was warmly welcomed. He later admitted that he was made to feel so much a part of the group that he had second thoughts about what he had come to do.

At his arraignment, family members appeared in the courtroom. Speaking directly to the accused, each spoke of their pain and, miraculously, their forgiveness. Nadine Collier, the daughter of one of the victims, church sexton Ethel Lance, said, "I forgive you. You took something very precious away from me. I will never get to talk to her again—you hurt me. You hurt a lot of people. If God forgives you, I forgive you."[6] The granddaughter of retired pastor Daniel Simmons spoke for many of the grieving families when she thanked the court for making sure hate doesn't win: "Although my grandfather and other victims died at the hands of hate, this is proof: everyone's plea for your soul is proof that they lived in love and their legacies will live in love."[7]

The day after the killings, the church was opened as usual for prayer and counseling. Despite the distrust between law enforcement and minority communities in many cities, the Emanuel community worked with Charleston police to avoid any demonstrations that could have led to violence and bloodshed.

"Mother Emanuel," as the church is known throughout Charleston, was formed by slaves in 1816. Its original church was burned to the ground by whites fearing a slave rebellion, but a new church—and a stronger community—rose from its ashes in 1834. When all-black church gatherings were banned during the dark days of the Civil War, services continued at Emanuel in defiance of such unjust laws. During the Civil Rights movement, Dr. Martin Luther King Jr. preached from its pulpit, and marches began from its steps.

When confronted with such horror and hatred, Mother Emanuel remembered what it means to be a church: to be ministers of reconciliation for a broken world, to be mirrors of God's grace in our midst, to be the means for healing despite our own pain, to be bread for those who hunger for peace and justice.

Jesus' Gospel lives at places like Mother Emanuel.

A good homily begins with praying the gospel—but a specific kind of prayer: "mulling" over the text. So let the pericope that will be the center of your homily become a prism to see your life unfold this week, and consider:

- What is the single most striking word, sentence, or image in this gospel?

- Where and how do we see this gospel in our time and place?

- What is Jesus asking us to do?

- How does this gospel reveal God's love in our midst?

Each of the examples cited above is the result of a homilist's "mulling." You might read those same gospel texts and be struck by an entirely different word or phrase or discover another idea or image revealing the love of God in our midst. That's the wonder and treasure of the gospels.

Typically, one or two key ideas will emerge from your "mulling." Your struggling to answer any of these questions is the beginning of preaching a homily that makes the Word of God "take flesh" for your parish community.

Communicaré

In the Benedictine tradition, there is a practice called *lectio divina*— "sacred reading." Each day, the monastic sets aside time to read, ponder, and pray over a (usually short) passage of Scripture. The passage is read slowly; each word and phrase is considered until the "voice" of God is heard, calling attention to a particular image or idea. From that word or phrase comes the monastic's prayer for grace, for direction, for peace.

There are four basic steps in *lectio divina*:

- reading: "What does this text say?"

- meditation: "What does this text say to me?"

- prayer: "What do I want to say to God through this text?"

- contemplation or action: "What difference might this text make in my life?" [8]

Begin the practice of *lectio* each week with the Sunday gospel. Set aside some time each week (whether you are preaching or not) to read the week's gospel. After your reading, consider the four questions posed above or the four questions discussed in this chapter:

- What is the single most striking word, sentence, or image in this gospel?

- Where and how do we see this gospel in our time and place?

- What is Jesus asking us to do?

- How does this gospel reveal God's love in our midst?

You might consider beginning a journal, making note of answers and observations from your *lectio* that may turn out to be the beginning of a future homily.

CHAPTER 4

One

Scene one: A wrecked automobile is being hoisted onto a trailer at the scene of a serious accident. The car is totaled. Releasing the car to the tow-truck driver, the trooper says, "They lived."

Scene two: The tow-truck driver delivers the car to the junkyard. The worker at the gate has seen these horrors before and instinctively assumes the worst. But the driver says, "They lived."

Scene three: The family who survived the crash climbs into their new car—the same make and model and color as the mangled wreck. "We lived, thanks to our Subaru," says the dad.

And the ad ends with Subaru's long-running tagline: *Love. It's what makes a Subaru, a Subaru.*

This memorable commercial is based on true stories from Subaru owners who say that their Subaru saved their lives or that of a loved one in a crash. And the vehicle seen in the spot is an actual wreck from which the driver survived.[1]

Reliability, comfort, design—every car maker can tout so many qualities about their vehicles. But in this spot, Subaru focuses on one message: the safety of their cars. And that message is centered on one image, the wrecked car, and one phrase, "They lived." The ad brilliantly gets the message across to viewers: Subaru is the safest car on the road.

One.

The homilist runs through his checklist every Sunday:

The key quote from the day's gospel, *check*. An explanatory word about the first reading, *check*. A brief note about what the apostle Paul is going on about in the second reading, *check*. A reminder about the second collection, *check*. Mention the bishop's letter in the bulletin, *check*. That story in the paper that caught his attention this week, *check*. The new adult religious program, *check*. The fundraiser for the youth group, *check*.

That's a lot for 10–12 minutes.

Jesuit Father John Conley calls this tendency to squeeze as much as possible into the homily "the Magellan sermon": "In the space of 20 minutes, the congregation is treated to a tour of the world as the preacher unloads a catalogue of random, unrelated thoughts."[2]

Or too many homilies operate like an old pinball game: the preacher furiously manipulates the levers to keep the marble hitting as many bells and whistles to run up the score of ideas as high as possible. At best, the Magellan and pinball approaches mirror Jesus' parable of the sower: "sow" as many ideas as you can and hope that something takes root in the minds and hearts of the congregation.

But more often than not, the reaction from the community is, *What was the point of all that?*

The reality is that your worshiping community hungers for one, clear, sustained insight into the gospel. They want to know how this gospel, this Scripture reading, this celebration, reveals the love of God in their lives. They hope that what they hear on Sunday will be experienced on the other six days of the week.

One.

An effective homily is centered on a single idea. After you pray and study ("mull" over) the Scriptures for Sunday, what's the one idea that strikes you? What's the one critical message you hear Jesus saying in this gospel? What is the most striking thing you see in this pericope from this story of Jesus' life?

There may very well be several ideas that get you thinking, that move you, that currently reverberate through the *zeitgeist*. Think and pray about them.

Then decide on which one to develop.

One.

Many of our teachers and professors instructed us to write a "thesis statement" for our essays and papers: a single, clear sentence that articulated precisely what we were trying to convey in this paper, the main idea that we wanted the reader to take away from our essay.

So what is Jesus' "thesis statement" in this gospel passage? What is the one main idea you hear Jesus saying in this text? There may well be several ideas or approaches to the main point in a given reading. That's the richness of Scripture—but, on this day, at this moment, in this community, what single idea speaks to your head and heart?

Once you realize that one point and can articulate it in *one* simple, clear sentence, write it down—and keep it in front of you as you assemble the homily:

> Every one of us has been entrusted with some kind of cross to carry that can be the means of resurrection.

> As this bread becomes the sacrament of Christ's Body for us, we must become the Body of Christ for one another.

> As Jesus reaches out to Peter when he falls below the waves, Jesus extends his hand to us in the hands of others.

> To truly follow Jesus begins by embracing his spirit of humility.

One.

When advertising agencies begin work on a new campaign for a client, the primary question the creative team asks at the outset is this: *What do we want the audience to do?* And they think in terms of a specific *verb*: to buy, to vote for, to call, to respond. They realize that they have a fixed number of seconds or a defined amount of space on the page or screen to persuade the audience to do that. Every second, every inch, every pixel counts.

The same is true for the homilist. You may go and on, but you will have your community's attention for just so long before they tune out. So what's the *one* thing you want them to take away from your homily into their real world of Monday through Saturday? What's the *one* thing you want them to do or what is the single response you seek?

One.

The previous chapter focused on four questions to "mull" and pray over as you begin your homily preparation. As you read the assigned gospel text, consider:

- What is the single most striking word, sentence, or image in this gospel?

- Where and how do we see this gospel in our time and place?

- What is Jesus asking us to do?

- How does this gospel reveal God's love in our midst?

Where have you seen this gospel in play in your life, in your family, in your parish? When have you heard Jesus articulating these words in your interactions with others and speaking these words in decisions you have had to make? What is this gospel saying to you, in the context of this solemnity or season? Where have you experienced the struggle and tension recounted in this gospel in your life? When have you realized the wisdom of Jesus' words and actions here in your journey? Where and when have you met the people we encounter in this gospel?

In your "mulling" and prayer, one answer to one of these questions will come to the surface of your consciousness. One answer will capture your imagination.

And that's the one idea you will make the center of your homily this Sunday.

One.

The homily is about revealing the love of God in the presence of the community; to preach the gospel is to show the way to follow Jesus in this time and place of ours.

To Make "One"

Focusing on one idea affects the structure of the homily as a whole. An effective homily has a unity, a "oneness" to it: a single idea or theme that is expressed in a unified structure.

The following homily illustrates this idea of "oneness" of structure. The homilist's text is the parable of the itinerant workers who are hired at different times of the day: some work a full day in the vineyard and some work only an hour—but at the end of the day, all receive the same wage (Matt 20:1-16a; the gospel for the 25th Sunday in Ordinary Time, Year A). In his "mulling" over the gospel, the homilist was struck by the first workers' need to have "more" for the sake of having more, despite their agreement to the original fair wage. Note the single theme carried throughout the piece: the idea of having enough—and the rhetorical devices employed to unify the theme.

The homilist begins with a story told by author Kurt Vonnegut in his commencement address at Rice University (May 9, 1998):

The late Kurt Vonnegut,
the author of such acclaimed novels as *Slaughterhouse-Five* and *Breakfast of Champions*,
told this story in a commencement address at Rice University:

Vonnegut was invited to a lavish party
thrown by a multibillionaire on his estate on Long Island.
At the party, Vonnegut caught up with his friend Joseph Heller,
    author of the novel *Catch-22*, one of the most popular books of all time.

As the two old friends were enjoying cocktails in this very opulent setting,
Vonnegut asked Heller:
"Joe, how does it make you feel to realize that only yesterday
our host probably made more money than *Catch-22* has grossed
    worldwide over the past 40 years?"

Heller smiled. "But I have something he can never have."

"What's that, Joe?"

"The knowledge that I've got *enough*."

Vonnegut then told the Rice graduates:
"[Heller's] example may be of comfort to many of you . . . who in later years
    will have to admit that something has gone terribly wrong—
that, despite the education you received . . .
you have somehow failed to become billionaires.
This can happen to people who are interested in something
    other than money, other than the bottom line."

And Vonnegut concluded: "We call such people *saints*—or I do . . ."

The homilist then connects Vonnegut's story to Jesus' point in that day's gospel by providing "snapshots" of God's presence in the lives of the worshiping community. In these real, authentic images, the community recognizes this gospel in their everyday reality:

To realize that we have *enough*—
that's the challenge of today's gospel.

No question, it's a struggle for all of us to make ends meet—
mortgages and groceries and tuition payments and keeping our cars on the
      road
take just about every shekel we have.
But there will *always* be one more thing we just *have* to have—
the newest, the latest, the biggest, the coolest.
If only I had such and such, life would be perfect.

No, it won't.

Because then there will always be something *else* you have to have . . .
and something new after that . . . and after that . . .
Satisfied? Not in this lifetime.
But more than *enough.*

Different examples—but they all illustrate the one, central idea of this homily: that we find our lives' true meaning and satisfaction not in things but in the values of God.

    The homilist concludes:

Today's gospel calls us
to shift the focus away from what we *don't* have
and be aware and grateful for what we *do* have:
    a loving family,
    good friends,
    a warm home,
    food on our tables,
    opportunities to learn, to work,
    to do meaningful and purposeful things in our lives.
Maybe not billionaire chic—but it's more than a lot of people have.

To possess such a sense of gratitude to God,
to realize that we, indeed, have *enough*—
    in fact, often more than *enough*—
is the mark of discipleship, of faithfulness and, yes,
    (as Kurt Vonnegut says) of *sainthood.*

God has entrusted us with many gifts, talents, and blessings
not to accrue more for ourselves
but to use what we have for the good of others,

without counting the cost or setting conditions or demanding a return.
And, when we stop and think about it,
it's *enough* . . .

Note the repeated use of the word *enough*. Its repetition throughout
the body of the homily keeps the central idea of the homily before the
listeners. Repeating a word or phrase in a speech is a classic rhetorical
device for focusing the audience's attention on the main idea. Martin
Luther King's iconic "I Have a Dream" speech at the March on Washington on August 28, 1963, is an example (italics added):

> *I have a dream* that one day this nation will rise up and live out the
> true meaning of its creed, "We hold these truths to be self-evident;
> that all men are created equal." *I have a dream* that one day . . . the
> sons of former slaves and the sons of former slave owners will be
> able to sit down together at the table of brotherhood. . . . *I have a
> dream* that my four little children will one day live in a nation where
> they will not be judged by the color of their skin but by the content
> of their character.
>
> *I have a dream* today!

Dr. King's repetition of the phrase "I have a dream" is an example of
anaphora—introducing a series of ideas with the same word or phrase.
The repetition of the phrase "I have a dream" makes King's vision
memorable and focuses clearly and sharply on what he has called the
assembled marchers to do. Dr. King's "dream" echoes in the hearts
and minds of a nation to this day.

The repetition of a word or phrase at the *end* of a series of consecu-
tive sentences is called *epistrophe*. The following is an example from
Walt Whitman's "Song of Myself" in *Leaves of Grass* (italics added):

> The moth and the fish eggs are *in their place*,
> The bright suns I see and the dark suns I cannot see are *in their place*,
> The palpable is *in its place* and the impalpable is *in its place*.

The apostle Paul's use of the word *child* in his First Letter to the Corinthians (13:11) is another example of epistrophe (italics added):

> When I was a *child*, I used to talk as a *child*, think as a *child*, reason
> as a *child*; when I became a man, I put aside *childish* things.

The three phrases of this passage from 1 Corinthians employ another rhetorical device: Each line is written in the same parallel structure: *talk* as a child, *think* as a child, *reason* as a child—verb followed by the prepositional phrase. Such *parallelism*—repeating a grammatical structure (be it a single word or a phrase) or following a consistent sentence structure (see the "Follow me" example below)—makes a point more memorable and visual to the hearer.

A homilist can create a similar effect. In the homily above, the word "enough" effectively connects the opening story, the discussion, and closing of the homily. Oh, it can easily be overdone; but when done carefully and strategically, the repetition of a word or phrase makes the *one* idea of the homily clear to the community—and helps the homilist stay focused, as well.

In preaching on some gospel texts, repeating the words of Jesus after a series of examples can effectively connect the principles of the gospel to the community's everyday reality. The words "Follow me" become an example of anaphora in this homily:

And Jesus said to one, *"Follow me."*

And he replied,
"I will *follow* you, Lord, right after I check the day's market reports."

But Jesus said,
"You cannot be my disciple if your concern for the poor and destitute does not match your concern for your portfolio."

Jesus said to another, *"Follow me."*

And she replied,
"I will *follow* you, Lord, right after I meet with my accountant to set up my 401(k)."

But Jesus said,
"You cannot be my disciple if your life's vision cannot see beyond the age of 66."

Jesus said to the teenager, *"Follow me."*

And the teen replied,
"I will *follow* you, Lord, as soon as I get back from soccer practice, meeting my friends at the mall, and updating my Facebook status."

But Jesus said,
"You cannot be my disciple if it's just another something on your
     schedule."

Jesus said to the mom and dad, *"Follow me."*

And the parents said,
"We will follow you, Lord, as soon as we are assured
that our child is loved and cared for."

But Jesus said,
"You cannot be my disciples until you realize
that to love and care for your child
is to be my disciple."

Note, too, the effectiveness of using the same sentence structure as
Luke does in his gospel (Luke 9:51-62).

A single word can be the unifier in the homily, making that word
the expression of the one idea. The word "signs" serves that function
in the following, preached on the First Sunday of Advent (Luke 21:25-
28, 34-36, Year C):

Signs:
Meteorologists watch a storm form in the middle of the Southern Atlantic.
They begin plotting the storm's course, entering data into their computers.
The computers then develop possible paths the storm may take
and the impact it could have in communities along the Eastern seaboard.
Warnings are issued—and people begin to get ready
for dangerous storms with disarmingly charming names like Sandy.

Signs:
Your son or daughter's mood has changed.
Your usually happy child is quiet, sullen, impatient, angry.
Typical teenage angst—
or is something deeper, more dangerous going on?

Signs:
At your annual checkup, the doctor sits you down.
He's concerned about the numbers on your chart.
He doesn't mince his words:
"You're over forty; you can't eat like a teenager anymore."

Throughout our lives, we encounter *signs:*
indicators of realities we do not readily see or understand or appreciate—
or would rather ignore altogether.

The conclusion is as critical to the homily's effectiveness as the open-ing visual. It's the coda to the message, the last note that resonates in the minds and hearts of the community.

Here's the conclusion to the homily on "enough." The preacher concludes with a story—and continues his use of the word "enough" to keep the focus on the central idea.

Note, too, the very last sentence. A well-crafted homily ends with a memorable "exit line" that embodies not only the theme but the tone of the homily—and, perhaps more important, ends on a positive note, a reason for hope in God's loving presence in our midst.

In our time and place, gratitude can be a hard virtue to embrace.

But thanks is not a mere sentiment—
It's an attitude . . .
It's an awareness of the bounty we have
and to realize the lunacy of frantic shopping for things that never satisfy . . .
Jesus' spirit of gratitude is to live our lives
not with a sense of entitlement—"Where's mine?"
but in humble awe of such a God
who breathes life into our being for no other reason than to give expression
　　to his inexplicably profound love.

To be a disciple of Jesus is to make gratitude our default position;
to follow Jesus is to seek to possess a constantly grateful heart.
At the end of the long work day, each one of us stands before God, humbly
　　and gratefully,
as his beloved sons and daughters.

And, when you think about it, that's more than *enough.*

And if you think it's *not* enough, consider this:
Just after World War II,
the pastor of a small parish announced
that a group of families who had all lost sons in the war
was donating money to buy a new baptismal font,

in memory of their fallen children.
A man sitting in the church turned to his wife and said,
"Maybe we should give, too."
His wife replied, "But our Danny came home from the war safe and sound."
"Exactly why," her husband said. "Exactly why."

May we find joy in the blessings of enough . . .

Enough said . . .

Pulpit Notes: **The Women of Good Friday**

An effective homily is *one* not only in idea but *one* in structure: All
the pieces work together as one—each sentence, each example, each
insight tied together in a clear, memorable conclusion. There is a unity
to the whole; there is a clarity, an easy-to-follow organization to the
homily that hearers can easily follow.

Note the organization and clarity of the following, preached by a
deacon on Good Friday. He reflects on the account of Jesus' passion and
death in the Fourth Gospel that had just been read (John 18:1–19:42):

> At the end, there were only four.
> Everyone else had fled.
> Besides the "beloved disciple," as the writer of the Fourth Gospel calls him,
> three women stand by Jesus' cross that terrible afternoon:
>> Jesus' mother;
>> Mary, the wife of Clopas, identified as the "sister" of Jesus' mother;
>> and Mary of Magdala (or Mary Magdalene).
>
> They stood there helplessly as their son and kinsman and friend hung there.
> They undoubtedly assisted with hasty burial arranged by Joseph of
>> Arimathea.
> They walked away from the garden together later that evening,
>> the mother supported by the other two.
>
> Each of these three women, in their own way,
>> shows us how to walk our own Good Fridays.

The homily's course has been set: walking this Good Friday with the
three women who keep vigil at the foot of the cross. The preacher leads
on:

Jesus' mother:

The mother of Jesus appears twice in John's gospel:
at the beginning of the gospel,
when she prevails upon her son to save the wedding feast at Cana,
and, today, when she is present at her son's execution.
For some reason, the writer of the Fourth Gospel never identifies her by
        name.
From the gospels of Matthew and Luke, we know her as Mary or Miriam.

From the moment of Jesus' birth,
she understood the life that lay before her son—
but that did not make this Friday any easier.
Though devastated,
she continued to trust that somehow
God would make something good come from her son's unjust
        and horrific death.
A mother's love never fails;
like the love of God, it knows no beginning or end.

On this Good Friday,
there are moms and dads anxious about the difficult times their sons and
        daughters are going through . . .
There are adult children keeping vigil at the bedside of a dying parent . . .
There are families this Good Friday
dealing with the crosses of unemployment, illness, separation,
        estrangement.
Like that of Jesus' mother, their love remains constant and complete.
Despite their fear for their children and loved ones,
despite their anxiety,
despite their sadness and distress over the rejection of their caring and
        outreach,
they struggle on,
refusing to abandon hope that their love will, somehow,
    transform this Good Friday into an Easter morning.
The mother of Jesus assures us that it can.

Note the structure: (1) a brief explanation of who the woman is and
what we know of her from Scripture; (2) what brings her to the cross;
and (3) how her experience parallels our own.

    The homilist continues his reflection with the second woman at
Jesus' cross:

Mary, the wife of Clopas:
The writer of the Fourth Gospel identifies her as Jesus' "mother's sister."
In gospel times, "sister" could indicate a number of relationships:
This Mary could be the blood sister of Jesus' mother;
she could also be Mary's cousin.
(Their having the same name wouldn't be all that unusual, either.)
Some scholars have suggested that Mary, the wife of Clopas, may have been
Mary's sister-in-law.

In any event, Mary the mother of Jesus and Mary the wife of Clopas are
family.

Note that the homilist does not go into a long, detailed exegesis here—
just what his hearers need to know to appreciate Mary of Clopas's
presence in the narrative.

Of the three Marys at the cross,
Clopas's Mary is probably most aware of how dangerous a place this is for
them to be.
But her sister's grief is her grief;
her sister's pain is her pain.
She would do anything to help her sister through her agony.
But all she can do is to be there for her and with her.
And that's enough.

We've all been this second Mary, the wife of Clopas:
We see family and friends going through a tough time,
and we want to do something to help, say something to reassure—
but we often don't know what that something is.
In our embarrassment and fear, we sometimes prefer to avoid the situation
altogether.
But, at such times, just being there is enough.
Just listening is enough.
Just reminding them that they are loved is enough.

That something is what Mary, the wife of Clopas, gives to her sister.
She stands with her sister and kin.
This is her family—they are the love of God in her life.
The selflessness and generosity of good folks like Mary of Clopas
are the first lights of Easter dawn . . .

The same pattern continues in the homilist's meditation on the "third Mary": who this Mary is, what brings her to the cross, and how her story helps us cope with our own Good Fridays.

Mary of Magdala:
The gospels give different accounts of exactly what happened,
but all agree that Mary, from the village of Magdala,
was healed of some serious affliction or illness by Jesus.
And from that moment of healing on,
Mary Magdalene led the company of women who followed Jesus and tended
    to his needs.
Jesus gave the Magdalene's life a hope and a purpose,
    a dignity and respect that she had never known before . . .
and she refused to surrender that hope—
    even at the foot of his cross.

Mary Magdalene's trust in God,
her faith in what she has seen of God's love in her life,
enables her to continue to hope and believe.
Although she doesn't get it yet,
she will understand what many of us have experienced:
that our real crosses are *not* instruments of death,
but the means to fulfillment and meaning and purpose in our lives;
that, as Jesus said in the gospel two Sundays ago,
only if the grain of wheat falls to the ground and dies
    will it realize its harvest.

That stubborn, nagging hope of Mary Magdalene
will bring her to the tomb on Sunday morning
and she becomes the first to announce the extraordinary news
    of the empty tomb . . .

The homily's conclusion serves as a final unifier of its one theme and the single focus of its structure:

On this Good Friday, we gather at the cross of Jesus
in the company of the three Marys.
May we come to see this Good Friday
and all the Good Fridays of our own lives

through the eyes of these three remarkable women:
>   with trust in the love of God to heal and re-create;
>   with steadfast compassion for family and friends
>   in whom we experience the love of God in our midst;
> with constant hope
>   that every cross we take up with humility and generosity
>   will bring us to Easter morning.

Communicaré

Take a look at the last homily you preached—and consider the following:

What was the single most important idea you wanted to get across? What secondary ideas or points got in the way, that detracted from the *one* point you wanted to make?

Underline the visual "snapshots" in this homily: real examples of how the gospel you were preaching on are seen and heard in the everyday lives of your community.

Did you employ any repetition devices that unified the homily's theme and structure? If not, could you have increased the memorability of your message by doing so? How?

Revisit the conclusion of this homily. Does it clearly articulate the *one* main idea you wanted to get across? How could you have made the conclusion a more effective means of unifying the homily?

CHAPTER 5

Preaching *Visually*

Can your community actually *see* what you're talking about on Sunday?

Certainly they *hear* the words of your homily. But can they *see* the Gospel in their lives? Can they imagine the love of God in their midst? Do they envision themselves in the role of prophet or disciple as Jesus calls us all to be?

The reality is that we live in a visual world. We are bombarded every day with pictures and images in the sharpest and most dramatic technologies. Most of us cannot function without our personal electronic devices. Too many of us live at our computer screens, high-definition televisions, and game consoles. And the use of PowerPoint, once considered a cool "special effect" for business presentations, has become *de rigueur* in conference rooms and classrooms.

Communications research has found that a speaker who incorporates some visual element in his or her speech or presentation is 40 percent more persuasive; an audience that can *see* what a presenter is proposing (whether a slick PowerPoint or "low-tech" dry-erase whiteboard) is twice as likely to be persuaded to embrace the presenter's position. And it has been shown that audiences retain five times more information when they can "see" it; while an audience typically comprehends about 10 percent of what they hear, they comprehend almost 90 percent of what they *see*.

But this "new" visualization has also had a negative effect on an audience's ability (and willingness) to pay attention. We get bored easily. We make a decision to stay tuned in to—or tune out entirely—a message within seven seconds. Those who teach at the college level long ago made peace with the fact that the fifty-minute stand-up lecture is deadly, that each succeeding generation of students is less and less able to focus on a single, detailed message for very long. Today's college students are used to quick, colorful, highly visualized bites of information before moving on to the next experience.

Now this is not to suggest that homilists "preach" from PowerPoint slides or use props at the ambo. But homilists today need to preach in a more *visual* language. The challenge for the homilist is to make the Gospel visible to the worshiping community: to make them *see* the reality, the good, the wisdom of the Word of God we proclaim.

Homilists can no longer speak in a theological "shorthand" and assume that today's congregations can decode words like *salvation*, *incarnation*, and *grace*. Understanding a phrase like "the mercy of God" or "the peace of Christ" cannot be taken for granted. Congregations want to know what that mercy and peace look like.

At the end of too many homilies, worshiping communities are left asking, *So?*

Today's struggling Christians long to experience God's mercy in their lives and work. The homilist's role is to reveal how that mercy is experienced in the mess and meanderings of everyday life.

They have to *see* what you're talking about.

Worshiping communities have to be able to "see" the preacher's point in stories and images that are centered in *their* experience, not the preacher's. We do not live in absolutes; our lives are far more complex than theological concepts. We live lives that are an ongoing struggle to make all the pieces fit into a meaningful whole. And we believe—we hope—in the depths of our hearts that the love of God is the connecting tissue between those parts.

Looking for the Gospel in Your Day

As discussed above in the essay "Four Questions," a key question the homi-list needs to answer as he or she thinks about a given gospel peri-cope is, *Where do I see this gospel taking place in the life of my community?*

Where do I see the forgiveness of the prodigal's father?

Where do I see the grain of wheat dying to itself to become something greater?

Where do I see Jesus carrying his cross?

What does this gospel mean to me as a parent? as a working man or woman? as a spouse? as a student?

How is this gospel lived in the kitchen? in the school yard? in the office?

Preachers and homilists often speak in the theological jargon of Scripture and doctrine. We have been articulating such formulae for so long it is presumed that the congregation shares our appreciation of the truth behind them; but, in fact, they are asking the very legitimate question, *What does this mean to me and my life?*

The beliefs of our creed are easy to list—but why do we believe those articles and what do those beliefs have to do with our everyday struggles?

The homilist's challenge is to help the community *see* that.

And that begins by the homilist seeing God's mercy, grace, and redemption in the households, workplaces, classrooms, and marketplaces where we live and work.

Consider the gospel for Holy Thursday: the Fourth Gospel's moving account of Jesus washing the feet of the Twelve. Think about how Jesus' *mandatum* is practiced in our time and place. Who are the "footwashers" you have encountered? Who are they and what drives them?

Here's what one preacher "sees":

At first, she refused to believe the doctor's diagnosis.
There must be some mistake.
She resolved to carry on her life as if nothing was wrong,
thumbing her nose at her illness;
but she soon conceded that the cancer was destroying her strength and
       energy.
She cried for days.
For a long time she closed herself off from others,
angry at God, angry at the doctors, angry at everyone.
Then came a desperate period of grasping at every possible cure,
from mysterious herbs to miraculous novenas.

But she eventually found within herself
the courage to accept what was happening
and the faith to place her life in God's hands.

That's when the transformation took place—
she, who could do less and less for herself physically,
became the caregiver.

Those who cared for her were buoyed by her faith and her sense of peace;
they felt a new pride and sense of purpose in their work
because of her encouragement.
Those who came to cheer her up
were the ones who left lifted up by her serenity and optimism.

She became a wellspring of love and peace for her family and friends.
From her small room, she dedicated herself to the work of the heart:
being reconciled with those from whom she had been separated,
preserving a lifetime of memories for her children and grandchildren.

Oh, there were many hard, painful days—
days when she longed for it to end.
But her generosity of spirit transformed her illness into a season of grace.
She embraced the spirit of the *mandatum.*
She had become a footwasher in the spirit of Jesus.

This courageous woman modeled for the homilist the "footwasher"
of the gospel: she bravely put aside her own "cloak" of fear and anger
and control to "bend down" and "wash the feet" of those around her.
The homilist saw in her a spirit of humility and selflessness, of respect
and love for others, that is required of those who would imitate Jesus
the footwasher.

The homilist recognized the spirit of the *mandatum* in her—and
helped his community see it as well.

So begin your homily preparation by looking around and seeing
your life and parish and world through the prism of the gospel. Translate what you see through that prism into colorful, vibrant words—and
share the pictures on Sunday morning.

Story: *Step Inside . . .*

The homiletic challenge is to learn to speak in the language of *story,*
image, and *metaphor.*

Scripture is filled with stories that teach and illuminate. Stories are
about change: in a good story, an individual is confronted with some
challenge that demands a response or action from him or her. A story
chronicles the individual's journey of discovering how to respond to
the challenge; in resolving the issue, the individual experiences a last-
ing change in attitude, understanding, and perception.

In every good story, we see ourselves in the place of the protagonist and wonder how we would respond to that challenge—sometimes readers and hearers will carry on a running argument with the protagonist as the character decides what to do (*No, don't go in there! How can you trust her? I bet he did it*). As we listen to Jesus' parable of the prodigal son, for example, we relate to one, if not all three, of the three characters as the parable unfolds. We have all been, at some point in our lives, the prodigal wanting to take on life on our own terms; we have been the father, worrying about those we love and fearing for their safety; and we have all been the resentful brother who has had enough of the selfishness and irresponsibility of our younger brothers and sisters.

The following story challenges its hearers to see faith as more than just word and ritual:

Many years ago there was a Japanese priest of the Zen religion.
The priest's name was Tetsugen.
Tetsugen had an idea:
to have the great teachings printed in the Japanese language for all to read
    and study.
So he assembled the ancient texts, translated them into Japanese,
and then traveled the length and breadth of Japan to solicit funds for the
    project.
Occasionally he would receive a gift as large as a hundred pieces of gold
from a wealthy landowner or merchant;
but mostly he received small coins from peasants.
The priest expressed equal gratitude to each donor, regardless of the amount.

After ten long years of travel,
the priest finally collected the funds necessary
to begin the time-consuming work of printing the book.
But just as the engravings were about to begin,
a great flood destroyed the homes of thousands of people.
So Tetsugen used the money he had collected for his cherished project
to help those left homeless and starving from the flood.

Tetsugen then began, again, the long, hard task of raising the funds
for his book of the great teachings.
Again he spent many years traveling throughout Japan soliciting the money
    needed for the printing.

But when the engraving was to start a second time,
a great epidemic swept through the land.
The priest used all the money he had collected to buy medicine
for the sick and dying.

A third time Tetsugen set out to raise the needed funds.
Almost thirty years later, his dream of a book of the great teachings,
written in Japanese, was finally realized.

The printing blocks that produced the edition are on display in a monastery
    in Kyoto.
The Japanese tell their children that the old priest Tetsugen actually "wrote"
    three editions of the great teachings:
the first two are invisible—and far superior to the third.

The timeless wisdom of the prophets, the great teachings of Jesus in
the gospel, are taught most eloquently and perfectly in acts of compassion and mercy. If we understand the depth of God's great love for us,
if we have any sense at all of what the death and resurrection of his
Son mean to us, then we cannot help but embrace his same Spirit of
love—love that is unconditional and selfless, love that gives joyfully
and gratefully.

The story of Tetsugen helps us *see* our baptisms in that light.

Most parents will immediately embrace the following experience
of a first-time father, recounted in one Sunday homily:

Sean arrived six weeks early:
"a tiny little gift from God,
a preemie whose heart and respiration rates would require extra monitoring,"
so Mom and Dad hunkered down for an extended hospital stay.
Ten days after his birth, something was wrong.
Sean's heart was not regulating the flow of blood properly.
Surgery was required—and immediately.
The next available slot was the following day.
The parents absorbed the news
and took turns holding vigil that night next to their infant son.
Mom took the first shift.
Dad "went to the family waiting area,
took two bites of a muffin and proceeded to stare blankly at it"
for what seemed like an eternity.

Dad remembers:

"I became aware of a couple sitting near me;
they were parents as well, and their little boy was across the hall from Sean.
I could not muster a smile, never mind the usual pleasantries.

"I did not know it at the time,
but these parents,
along with the other families in the cardiac intensive care unit,
would teach me more about parenting than any book possibly could.
It was here I found the patience and care of parents under incredible stress.
It was here I learned firsthand about the gift of new life
and just how fragile it can be.
It was here that I witnessed a kind of love that was altogether new to me.

"Later that day, a stuffed animal arrived
courtesy of the parents I met in the waiting area,
along with a card that welcomed us into the world of 'heart moms and dads.'
I became a silent admirer of this couple,
whose child had undergone multiple surgeries.
They were just across the hall,
and though I tried to give them privacy,
my gaze kept wandering in their direction,
peeking between the curtains to see how experienced parents handle
this sort of stress.
I could see they had it together.
They knew the purpose of each IV line and tube;
they asked the doctors spot-on questions."

Sean's surgery was a success.
"Unfortunately, his 'one and done' operation and excellent prognosis were
        not the norm. . . .
As [they] prepared to transfer out of the intensive care unit,
a feeling of guilt crept into [his parents'] sense of relief.
[Their] son was doing better, but so many children were still struggling.

"In my final conversation with the couple across the hall," Sean's dad writes,
"they could sense my mixed feelings.
Yet they were so positive and happy for us.

Rejoice in your son, they said, and pray for ours.

"In a place in which each child had a wounded heart,
we were overwhelmed by the love and generosity of strangers,
of 'heart moms and dads' who modeled the most important lessons to two
    new parents." [1]

In these "heart moms and dads" who console and teach, who rejoice and grieve with each other, who are bound together by that unconditional and complete love of a parent for a child, we "see" the kingdom of God. The kingdom of God, the homilist reflected, is not found in the world's centers of power but within human hearts; it is built not by deals among the brokers of that power but by the hands of faithful and generous souls; it is influenced neither by wealth nor status but by compassion, humility, and justice.

The kingdom of God can be *seen* in our midst in such generosity of heart and joyful humility. Tell these stories to your community on Sunday.

Image: *A Photo from Your Life*

While most preachers readily acknowledge the power of story, some shy away from taking on the role of storyteller, fearing that they lack the necessary performance skills to keep an audience enthralled.

But storytelling does not necessarily mean lengthy and detailed narratives with intricate plots and a full cast of characters. Good stories can be simple images and word-pictures that people know and see and feel. Sometimes a homily's story will have all the dramatic elements of plot, confrontation, climax, and resolution, or the comic setup leading to the well-timed punch line; often, however, a picture painted in words or the relating of a situation or experience common to everyone becomes a story that tells itself in the imagination of the listener. These simple images can reveal a faith that is just as real and meaningful as the most cleverly developed and entertainingly performed narrative. With the right image suggested by the homilist, listeners can tell their own stories within their own imaginations.

Another way to look at it:

A story is about *change*, a narrative that includes (to some degree) the devices of plot, characterization, conflict, climax, and resolution.

An image, however, is a snapshot, a moment in time in which we can see ourselves and identify with the situation and the challenges presented in that particular set of circumstances. The widow who gives her few pennies to God, the father trying to get his two sons to do their chores, the man who discovers the priceless pearl, seed scattered with persevering hope are all images that Jesus employs to help his hearers *see* what is meant by gospel generosity and justice.

A few weeks before the First Sunday of Advent, a homilist saw on television the return of a National Guard unit from Afghanistan and their joyful reunion with their families. The scene prompted this meditation on the Advent theme of waiting:

> A young wife and her infant daughter can barely contain themselves as they
> wait.
> Any moment now her husband's unit will march into the arena after a year
> in Afghanistan.
> They've talked every day via Skype,
> so at least she knew he had made it through another day;
> he saw images on his laptop of their little Sarah who was born after he left—
> he has yet to hold his daughter.
>
> The waiting began with the first word that his unit would be called up;
> the waiting took on new urgency as he made arrangements
> for the family's care during his absence.
> Waiting was part of the couple's everyday routine
> until they made their daily Skype connection—
> and if the call was late or delayed, the waiting became unbearable.
> Their waiting became expectation as the day approached
> when he would come home.
>
> Now, on this day they have been waiting for
> for what seems like an eternity,
> their eyes meet the moment he enters the arena.
> A few more minutes for the formal dismissal. . . . wait, wait, wait.
> And the long wait melts when husband and father,
> wife and mother,
> and beautiful daughter are in one another's arms again.

They go home,
happily awaiting the next chapter of their life together as a family.

Such agonizing waiting is a reality for many military families. The season of Advent teaches us that waiting is often the cost of love: In waiting for someone, our everyday business becomes almost meaningless as we anticipate, worry, and prepare for their return. In waiting, we realize our own powerlessness; we realize our deepest hopes and needs; we realize the gift the person we are awaiting is to us.

Help your community "see" how and why we wait.

Many a preacher (not to mention teacher or workshop leader) has wanted to call out the individual whose cell phone rings in the middle of the homily or class. One homilist did (sort of), when he preached on the story of sisters Martha and Mary (Luke 10:38-42):

That's quite a little device you have there.
How long has it owned you?

It does, you know.
Because you're terrified of missing something.
It's the information age, after all.
Information is the gold standard.
Who's ahead, what's selling, what's new.
Gotta check your balance, available flights to Toronto,
your team's schedule, tomorrow's weather in Belize.

And you have to know. And you have to know *now*.

Because if you don't stay on top of it all . . .

Because if you miss a text . . .

Well, you just *have* to . . .

So you keep your nose pressed to that little screen.
At dinner. At school. Even (God help us all) while you're driving.
You can be *among* people—but you're not *with* them.
While you're in constant touch with texters and bloggers,
the person sitting right next to you,

your loved one who is trying to get your attention,
might as well be on the moon.

Don't think for a moment you're in control
    of this little electronic mechanism in your hand.
That little box of light is leading you, literally, by the nose.

You're worried and distracted by many things, Jesus says.
There is need of only one.

"Just one thing?
You've got to be kidding me, Jesus!
Don't you realize how much stuff is going on?
And how much I need to be on top of it all?
My life is on this phone!
But, you know, Jesus, you might have a point . . .
Oh, hold on, I've got a call on the other line and a text message that just
    came in.
I really have to take this.
Can I get right back to you, Jesus? Thanks.
Hold it—good, I got your picture for my Facebook page.
Oh, and Jesus, do you have an app?"

Oh, these are miraculous devices.
But are they really making our lives easier and more manageable—
or are *they* managing us?
Our smartphones and BlackBerrys and tablets and PEDs
mirror the Martha/Mary conundrum that every one of us faces:
trying to balance the day-to-day demands of everyday living
with the need to connect our souls to God and the things of God.

In the ubiquitous cell phone and the many personal electronic devices that rule our lives, we are confronted with choosing "the better
part" embraced by Mary: to "unplug" from the mundane and empty
pursuits of the everyday to realize, with gratitude, the presence of God
and the joy and love of family and friends.

In the meditation (rant?) above, the homilist presents a series of
images that those of us who live by our phones immediately recognize:
the need to be in constant touch, the fear of missing the latest, the

demand for immediate access to information, the embarrassment we experience when we realize how long we have ignored the people we are with because our faces and attention have been stuck to our screens.

In such images, we *see* the light.

Metaphor: *The Power of Everyday Things to Teach*

"The kingdom of heaven is like," Jesus begins many of his parables. Sometimes we can begin to see the deeper meaning of life in "like" things. Scripture is filled with beautiful metaphors: "The just shall flourish like a palm tree" . . . "The Lord is my shepherd" . . . "You are salt and light . . ."

Everyday events and things can help us realize the love of God in our lives. Jesus' comparing himself to a "gate" (John 10:1-10) led to this meditation on doors:

We pass through a great many doors in our lives.

The open door welcomes; it ushers in fresh air and light.
Yes, we're open, come on in, welcome!
The open door is the sure sign that we belong,
that we have a place,
that we are among those who love us.

The closed door shelters and protects us from the winter cold—
as well as from the intruder, the thief, the evildoer.
Come in out of the cold, you're safe here, everything's fine.
Behind the closed door we are safe and held close.

In any new construction,
architects spend a great deal of time and money designing the entry.
The size and colors of portals and thresholds
convey to the visitor authority, majesty, mystery, stature.
Passing through doors can intrigue us, excite us, inspire us,
fill us with awe or dread.
Locked doors are sure signs of defeat, rejection, desperation.

Doors can speak for us, as well.
They can be slammed in anger.

They can be opened in an act of compassion.
In the corporate world, just having a door
    indicates your place and status in the organization.
And in every community the real power rests with the one
    who has the key to the door.

The doors we pass through are transitions from fear to sanctuary,
from isolation to community,
from struggle to peace.

The church door welcomes us into God's presence.
The courthouse door is the entryway for procuring justice
    and protecting the common good.
The university door is the threshold of learning and discovery.
Our own front door is the blessed assurance that we are home.

In John's gospel, Jesus calls himself the "gate," the entryway, for us to God, the "door" through which we step from our imperfect, incomplete world to the perfect holiness of God. God invites us to pass through the threshold that is his risen Christ: to leave behind our sadness and fears and doubts in order to come into the safety and warmth of God's hearth of peace and compassion. On our journey to the kingdom of God, Jesus is the "gate" of humble justice, selfless compassion, and ready forgiveness that leads us to the dwelling place of God.

The metaphor of the door helps us *see* that the Jesus of the gospels is that entryway in our everyday passages and walkways.

A Good Friday reflection offered this meditation on the "crosses" we bear everyday—that we often don't even realize we have taken up:

It may be the mountain of laundry you face every day
or your child's tuition bill.
It could take the form of the textbooks you use to teach your students,
the tools and equipment you operate at the construction site,
the computer that produces the reports and graphics that keep your business
    humming along.
Yours may be the soup you make and serve at the local soup kitchen
or the soccer ball you use to coach a team of excited six- and
    seven-year-olds.

Some of the most beautiful ones
are the ear that is always ready to listen to another's troubles,
the shoulder always available for a loved one to cry on,
the smile that readily comforts,
the heart that never fails to break with another.
Believe it or not, spouses are sometimes big ones for the other;
good friends readily accept each other as one.

They are all crosses.

We tend to think of crosses as burdens, things—and people!—
that demand so much energy and time from us.
We see our sufferings and our brokenness as "crosses"
that condemn us to living incomplete and unfulfilled lives of sadness and
        despair.
Many days we would like to lay those crosses aside
and never pick them up again.
But our real crosses—
the crosses God places on our shoulders and Christ bears with us—
are sources of hope, of joy, of discovery, of life, of resurrection—
    for both others and ourselves.
They are not the limitations of our lives
but the means to living our lives to the fullest,
the vehicles for discovering the meaning and purpose of this journey that
        God has set us on.

Today we remember the day Jesus,
in a spirit of obedience and love,
took up his cross.
Clearly, our crosses pale in the shadow of his.
But, as the wood of his cross becomes the tree of Easter life,
our crosses, when taken up in his spirit of humility and compassion,
can be no less than the first light of Easter dawn.

In common everyday things and experiences, in the light of faith, we
can see God in our midst. Your homily can and should be that light.

Preaching visually requires a special awareness, a spirituality centered in the common and everyday, a sense of pastoral understanding

grounded in the experience and faith of the people the homilist has been called to serve. It requires a faithfully tuned ear and a compassionately grounded lens to behold God present in every offering of forgiveness, in every act of kindness, in every moment of selfless love and humble generosity.

John the Baptizer in the Fourth Gospel models this challenge. While the camel skin–clad Baptizer in the Synoptics is the hammer of God admonishing his hearers to reformation and conversion, the John portrayed in the Fourth Gospel is a much more approachable and reconciling figure. The writer of the Fourth Gospel presents John as a voice of hope and joy who dedicates himself to giving testimony to the "light." The self-effacing John of the Fourth Gospel goes to great lengths to minimize his role in order to enable the people of the Jordan region to recognize the Christ walking among them.

Look, he says, *there is the Lamb of God in your midst, right there in your life.*

John does not speak in dogmas and concepts; he points to God living in our midst. In the Fourth Gospel, the Baptizer is the welcoming entryway for many to "behold" the Lamb of God in their midst. John opens the hearts and spirits of those who come to his baptism to the first light and hope of the Messiah.

In every act of selfless generosity and humble compassion, the Lamb of God walks in our midst. The preacher/homilist has been called, as the Baptizer was called, to point to the Christ, the Lamb of God, dwelling among us and walking with us in our doubts, our hurts, our fears.

Help us *see* Christ in our midst.

Communicaré

Read the gospel for this Sunday. Over the next few days, keep the point of the gospel in mind as you read or watch the news (on whatever device you use) or stream movies and television programs. Note anytime you "see" that gospel in the stories and images you encounter.

Keep a notebook or computer file and make a note whenever you *see* a sign of God's presence and grace in your everyday travels. The more mundane and ordinary, the better. Simplicity is key here. Every few weeks, rummage through your notes. In the light of the gospel readings of the season, are there stories here to share?

CHAPTER 6

Putting It Together

In chapter 12 of Luke's gospel, Jesus is asked to settle a dispute between the two brothers over an inheritance. Jesus refuses to involve himself in the matter, warning the brothers and the assembled crowd to "guard against all greed, for though one may be rich, one's life does not consist of possessions" (v. 15).

Which prompts Jesus to tell the following parable:

> "There was a rich man whose land produced a bountiful harvest. He asked himself, 'What shall I do, for I do not have space to store my harvest?' And he said, 'This is what I shall do: I shall tear down my barns and build larger ones. There I shall store all my grain and other goods and I shall say to myself, "Now as for you, you have so many good things stored up for many years, rest, eat, drink, be merry!"' But God said to him, 'You fool, this night your life will be demanded of you; and the things you have prepared, to whom will they belong?'" (vv. 16-20)

Jesus then articulates the point of his story:

> "Thus will it be for the one who stores up treasure for himself but is not rich in what matters to God."
>
> "Therefore I tell you, do not worry about your life and what you will eat, or about your body and what you will wear. For life is more than food and the body more than clothing. Notice the ravens: they do not sow or reap; they have neither storehouse nor barn, yet God feeds them. How much more important are you than birds! Can any of you by worrying add a moment to your lifespan? If even the smallest

things are beyond your control, why are you anxious about the rest? Notice how the flowers grow. They do not toil or spin. But I tell you, not even Solomon in all his splendor was dressed like one of them. If God so clothes the grass in the field that grows today and is thrown into the oven tomorrow, will he not much more provide for you, O you of little faith? As for you, do not seek what you are to eat and what you are to drink, and do not worry anymore. All the nations of the world seek for these things, and your Father knows that you need them. Instead, seek his kingdom, and these other things will be given you besides." (vv. 21-31)

Jesus then concludes his "homily" with words of hope:

> "Do not be afraid any longer, little flock, for your Father is pleased to give you the kingdom. Sell your belongings and give alms. Provide money bags for yourselves that do not wear out, an inexhaustible treasure in heaven that no thief can reach nor moth destroy. For where your treasure is, there also will your heart be." (vv. 32-34)

Jesus employs this "structure" many times in the gospels: he begins with a parable or picture drawn from the everyday lives of his listeners, then explains how the story or image reveals the presence of God in their lives; he concludes his "homily" with a word of hope or a call to act or change in order to embrace God's love in their everyday lives.

In high school and college speech classes, students are taught Aristotle's structure of effective rhetoric: an introduction to the topic, three main points clearly defined and organized, and a conclusion summarizing the material. Many preachers follow Aristotle's model. Sometimes included, mostly out of a sense of obligation (if this is going to be a *real* homily, after all), is some exegetical background on the three readings and an admonition to the congregation to either stop doing something or start doing something.

But consider for a moment not only the teaching of Jesus but the teaching *method* of Jesus. Jesus' words, especially his parables, are masterpieces of thoughtful, concise, and meaningful communication. Jesus' preaching typically includes three elements:

1. The *story* or *image* from the everyday world of his hearers. The story visualizes for the listener some truth about the kingdom of God: God's loving presence in our midst—hidden, perhaps, but still very real.

2. The *connection* between that story and the reality of God's love in our time and place—how the holy is ever present in the most unexpected of places.

3. The *invitation* to embrace that love, to realize that presence in our lives.

These three elements are all at work in the parable above. A rich man becomes so obsessed with his possessions and wealth that he begins a massive building project of bigger storage units (before we get too self-righteous here, maybe we should first take a look at our garages and basements or count the number of closets in our houses). But the rich "fool" dies unexpectedly and realizes that his vast holdings mean nothing in the economy of God (the *story*, vv. 16-20).

Jesus then asks the crowd (us) to consider how our own pursuit of wealth and our obsession with having the newest, the biggest, and the coolest can distract us from what is truly important and good in these lives God has given us (the *connection*, vv. 21-31). Note, too, that Jesus includes the additional images of the ravens and flowers to underscore the difference between what we *need* to live and what we *want*.

Jesus concludes his teaching with words of hope: not to be afraid to place our trust in the things of God—and calling us to share what we have with the poor to realize the "treasure" of God's kingdom in our own time and place (the *invitation*, vv. 32-34).

Though one could argue quite correctly that this approach "fits" the Aristotelian rhetoric model of introduction/three points/conclusion, the *story/connection/invitation* model takes a very specific approach to structuring and delivering a gospel-centered homily. Structuring the homily using this model can help many homilists think through and deliver a more effective, meaningful homily to their worshiping communities.

Story

The beauty of Jesus' parables is their ability to take the ordinary and, through them, reveal the extraordinary. Through stories about wayward children, lost coins, unexpected finds, paychecks, mustard seeds and weeds, Jesus makes the presence of God real for his hearers of every time and place.

We have all heard again and again (as in the previous chapter of this book) that storytelling is the most effective form of preaching. But storytelling does not necessarily mean long and detailed narratives with intricate plots and a full cast of characters. Good stories can be simply images that people know and see and feel. One of the foremost storytellers of our time, Garrison Keillor, the creator of NPR's *Prairie Home Companion*, says that a good story "allows people to come into it. You can somehow envision yourself as a participant in the story."[1]

As discussed in the last essay, a homily's story can have all of the dramatic elements of plot, climax, and resolution, or a carefully constructed comic setup leading to a well-timed punch line; but a homily's story can also be a simple image, a "snapshot" from our everyday lives that weaves its own story in the imaginations of listeners. An effective homily can be centered on a story recounting a challenge or change confronting a protagonist (the rich man building new grain bins)—or it can begin with a simple image in which the listener recognizes his or her own experience (the flowers of the field).

The right image or idea can trigger the listener's own story: personal experiences based on his or her own encounters with that image. From those "stories" a homilist can share faith that is meaningful and real.

Keep in mind that the homily's story is the entryway for the listener to the wisdom of that day's gospel. So start with the story—don't bury it in the middle of the homily. If you start your homily with an observation about the gospel reading and then hear yourself saying something like, "Today's gospel is like" and then begin relating a story or presenting an image, reverse the order. Start with the story or image (everything after "It's like . . ."), and then go into the explanation.

A deacon was preparing to preach on the parable of the prodigal son (Luke 15:11-31), read on the Fourth Sunday of Lent in Year C in the Sunday Lectionary cycle. In his "mulling" over this gospel he had heard many, many times before, he was struck this day by the scene in the pigsty, when the prodigal comes to his senses and realizes what a mess he has made of his life. From the scene in the pigsty, the deacon recalled a recent car trip with his wife—an experience that many couples know all too well:

> He and she are going to meet some friends for dinner at a restaurant just outside the city.
> As they're getting into the car, she offers him a piece of paper.

"Sheila e-mailed the directions to the restaurant."
He waves her off—and then speaks the immortal words:
"I don't need directions. I know exactly where I'm going."

And so off they go, heading down the highway toward the city.
The GPS is, of course, off.
She sees they're coming to the exit written on the directions,
but he continues on the highway.
"Wasn't that our exit, honey?" she asks.
He—being a "he"—insisted, "No, it isn't."
End of discussion.

They pass a second exit for the same town.
"I think Sheila said that . . . "
"Look, would *you* rather drive?"
She says nothing more.

They drive on . . . and on . . . and on . . .
"Maybe we should check the GPS," she suggests.
"We don't need it!" he snaps.
There is a long silence.
They continue on the highway.
Before long, they are beyond their destination
and are well on their way to the next major city.
And state.

"Honey?" she says.
There is a hint of panic in her voice.
But he keeps on, determined to prove her wrong.
He will find his way without turning around.

But after almost an hour and many miles later,
He finally hears that little voice inside of him that says:
"Give it up, Bozo. You're lost!"
And so, with great humility, he pulls over.

"Let me see the directions," he says, barely able to breathe.
He then turns around at the next exit.
She says nothing. She just places her hand on his.

Many people in the congregation have been on that car trip. Many of
the "guys" eventually confront their own stubbornness on that drive,

and the spouses in the congregation wish they had been as patient as the wife in the deacon's story.

While preparing to preach on the parable of the sheep and the goats (Matt 25:31-46, the gospel for the solemnity of Christ the King in Year A), a homilist came across the following story in an essay by Heidi Neumark, a Lutheran pastor in New York City, published in *The Christian Century*. The homilist went on to read more about this growing real estate practice in *The New York Times*.

This was the "story" he told that Sunday:

New York City is a very expensive place.
Many of us know that from our own travels to the "Big Apple."

Imagine trying to live there.
To give you some idea:
an apartment in Manhattan
with less square-footage than our cramped little choir loft
sells for more than a million dollars.

In order to provide affordable housing for the low-income, working poor,
the city of New York has set up the Inclusionary Housing Program.
Under the plan, construction companies and real estate developers are given
          generous subsidies and tax breaks
if their luxury buildings reserve a certain percentage of units for low-income
          families and tenants.
So far, so good . . .

But one developer's recent application included a unique—
and cynical—brand of social engineering.
In their proposed high rise,
the developer's plan includes the required units for low-income families—
but tenants residing in those affordable apartments
will have their own separate entryway—
in a back alley behind the building.

A spokesman for the company explained:
"No one ever said that the goal was the full integration of these
          populations. . . .
I think it's unfair to expect very high-income homeowners
who paid a fortune to live in their building

to have to be in the same boat as low-income renters,
who are very fortunate to live in a new building in a great neighborhood."[2]

I'm sorry to report that the city approved the company's plan for the "poor
    door."
And now other developers have begun adding similar separate entrances to
    their new buildings.
The "poor door."

Two stories—one from the everyday adventures of marriage and one
from the world of high-priced real estate—set the stage for revealing
God in our midst.

Connection

An insightful definition of the role of the homilist appears in the
1982 reflection *Fulfilled in Your Hearing: The Homily in the Sunday Assembly*, published by the US Bishops' Committee on Priestly Life and Ministry. The homilist's words, the bishops write, should "help people *make connections* between the realities of their lives and the realities of the Gospel . . . [and] help them see how God in Jesus Christ has entered and identified himself with the human realities of pain and of happiness."[3]

How succinctly and accurately put. This communication, an act of both liturgical prayer and ministry, should enable the community to see how Sunday's gospel "connects" to their Monday-through-Saturday world. Among the implications for the homilist, then, is the need to be in touch with that world. This is the ministerial dimension of homiletics: to love one's community enough to listen to them, to travel with them on their journeys, to honor their struggles to live faithfully in a world working overtime to diminish any sign of God's presence.

The second part of Jesus' homiletic model makes that connection—between the story we see and experience and the reality of God's presence in our lives that we often don't realize. In the homily on the story of the prodigal son, the homilist "connected" the story of the husband finally admitting he was lost to Jesus' iconic parable:

This little scene is really Jesus' story of the prodigal son—
the dynamics are the same.

Like the prodigal, our hero thinks he knows where he's going.
He refuses to accept what the signs are telling him:
that he's heading in the wrong direction.
Only when he faces the reality that he's lost and admits that he needs help
can he turn around.
Until he confronts his mistake, he's stuck in the mud—
like the prodigal in the gospel.

We've all had our "pigsty epiphanies":
We make a mess of things
and we cannot or refuse to understand how bad a mess we've made.
But eventually there comes that moment
when we can no longer deny how much hurt we've caused;
we reach the point when we can no longer stand the situation
and finally resolve to act, to change, to make better, to reconcile.

We realize how estranged we've become from ourselves and others.
We've had enough of being trapped in the prisons created by our arrogance
        and pride
and being buried in the tombs of fear that we've dug for ourselves.

In the parable of the prodigal son,
that realization takes place when the prodigal is reduced to tending the swine
and finally accepts responsibility for the disaster he has made of his life.
It's the beginning of his reconciliation with his father and family.
Forgiveness's only chance at sticking
depends on our realizing that we are in need of forgiveness
and that forgiveness (despite our doubts, insecurities, and egos) is possible.

During this season of Lent, we talk a lot about *conversion.*
And that's exactly what the word conversion means: *to turn around.*
Just as the foolish son, in the middle of the pig farm,
finally realizes he has to turn his life around and return to home,
just as the stubborn husband realizes he has to turn around if they're going
        to meet their friends,
God calls us each Lent to recalibrate our directions
and to turn around, as needed, to make our way to God.

Note that the preacher here does not just drop in the word *conversion*—
he explains it in terms that relate to his hearers' lives (as the homily

continues, he will also offer an insight into the meaning of forgiveness).
The homilist then makes another important "connection" between the
episode in the car and the two other characters in Jesus' parable:

Which brings us to "she."
As the scene unfolds, she has a choice.
She can be the prodigal's father . . . or the prodigal's older brother.
Let's face it:
We wouldn't blame her a bit if she let him have it:
His arrogance and stubbornness have made them late,
    have wasted hours of time,
    have all but ruined their night out.

Truth be told, we understand the older brother.
We get his anger. We've been the older brother:
No matter what we do for you, it isn't enough.
Time to grow up. Take responsibility for your actions. Get it together.
You want to make a train wreck out of your life, be my guest.
But I'm not bailing you out again.
I've wasted enough time with you.

Ever say that? Ever *wanted* to say that to someone?

But, if we're serious about following Jesus,
we have to be the prodigal's father—
we have to make it possible for the prodigal to *turn around.*
She does that for him in the car.
She certainly has every right to let him have it.
But she doesn't.
She knows this is a hard moment for him.
So she puts aside her anger and, by taking his hand,
    lets him know that it's OK to turn around.

The Greek word that we translate as "forgive"—*aphiemi*—means "to let go."
That's the heart of forgiveness: *letting go*—
letting go of the past so that both the forgiver and the offender can start over;
letting go of our need to control;
even letting go of our being right
so that something new and healing can happen in our lives and relationships.

That's the difference between the father and the older brother:

The father, because of his great love for both his sons,
is able to let go of his own hurt and welcome back his beloved wayward child.
Letting go of his disappointment and hurt
enables the father to rejoice in his son's return and the healing of his family.
The older brother, quite understandably, is angry at his younger brother—
but he will only be at peace when he lets go of that anger and resentment;
the family will only be a family again when he lets go of his need to somehow
        punish his brother.

Forgiveness does not negate the need for making things right;
reconciliation does not dismiss one's responsibility and accountability.
But to follow Jesus is to always, always, leave open the possibility
        for *turning around.*

To follow Jesus is to possess the humility to admit
when we're up to our necks in the mud.
To follow Jesus is to possess the humility to wade into that mud
        and pull someone out.

In the homily on the "poor door," the homilist makes clear that "separate entrances" are not just a trend in uptown New York real estate but a reality in our own time and place. Here's his "connection":

Sometimes, without even realizing it, we set up "poor doors"—
separate entrances
    for those we want to keep at a distance,
    for those we don't have time for,
    for those whose problems, whose issues, whose "dramas"
    we want no part of.

We prefer to deal with poverty—whatever form that poverty takes—
as an abstraction rather than a reality,
something "out there" somewhere far away from our own safe little world.
[Please use the poor door. Thank you for your cooperation.]

The fact is that Jesus himself enters our lives through such "poor doors."
In the kingdom of God, there are not front-door people and back-door people.

In the reign of Christ, we are all welcomed through the one front door,
we all have a place at the one table of heaven,
we all stand before the one God together, humbly and gratefully,
as children of the same Father.
The only door to the kingdom of God *is* the poor door.

In today's gospel, Jesus identifies himself with the "least of these"—
those who are hungry or thirsty or naked or sick or imprisoned,
those who are alone or lost or broken.
If we want to follow Jesus,
we have to bend down, squeeze through, hold our breath,
and follow him through the poor door.
And we have to leave our own wants and needs and egos outside
if we're going to make our way through.

Using the same sentence structure as Jesus' parable, the homily makes the connection clear and memorable to his community:

And when we do for the "least of these," Christ says,
    we do for Christ himself:
Christ is the infant you nurse at three a.m.
Christ is the six-year-old nervous about starting school.
Christ is the young adult you are struggling to put through college.
Christ is everyone sitting at your family table this evening.

When we say hello to that guy everybody thinks is weird,
we are greeting Christ.
When we prepare supper to take over to the sick neighbor,
we are caring for Christ.
When we offer a few dollars to help a struggling family make ends meet,
we are helping Christ.
When we make soup and sandwiches for the guests at the local soup kitchen,
we are serving Christ.

And such care and service to Christ is only by way of the poor door.

As disciples of Jesus,
we are called to make the kingdom of God a reality
in whatever place we are,

in whatever time we live.
God's reign is established,
not only by acts of heroic sanctity or miraculous transformations,
but by the simplest and most hidden offerings
of compassion, of reconciliation, of peace, of justice.
Discipleship begins with seeing
in every man, woman, and child the face of Christ,
and to then afford them the dignity and respect worthy of that identity.

And that means using the poor door.
There are no back entrances to the kingdom of God;
there are no private elevators to God's dwelling place.
Every entrance is a "service" entrance.

As Jesus does in Luke 12 above, the deacon/homilist includes a second image to reinforce the connection between our reality and the holy in our midst:

A final story:
When my wife Ann's mother was very ill,
a good friend of my mother-in-law went out of her way to be of help.
Lydia, kind and generous with typical self-effacing Midwestern graciousness,
would spend time with Ann's mom,
run errands, take care of housekeeping chores,
do whatever needed to be done to help.
But Lydia's own life was filled with hardships and struggles of her own.
One day Ann asked Lydia how she could be so generous with her time
when there were already so many other issues she was dealing with
within her own family.
Lydia said simply,
"But, Ann, doing these few things for your mom is a gift.
It gets me away from my own problems and thinking about someone else.
Your mother has been so kind to me and my family over the years.
Whatever I'm able to do for her, I offer as a prayer of thanks to God."

Today's gospel reimagined in a Minnesota kitchen . . .

Making such connections, focused on one clear idea or theme, reveal the presence of God in the midst of our ordinary, harried, seemingly

God-less lives. Considered thoughtfully and executed effectively, the second part of the homily lifts the gospel reading off the lectionary page and opens it up as an experience of God's wisdom and grace for listeners.

Invitation

Jesus' parable of the rich fool ended with an invitation to follow Jesus in his work of healing and reconciliation, to embrace the love of God in our midst, to take on the work of creating the kingdom of God here and now.

The conclusion can be the most challenging part of the homily—for both the community and the preacher. It should, first, be an invitation to hope: that the gospel opens us up to the possibilities to transform, to re-create, to heal. The conclusion should invite the community to realize the love of the always present, if sometimes hidden, God. While the homily's theme may confront us with the reality of the humility of the cross in our lives, it should end in the first light of Easter morning.

Sadly, too many homilies seem long on admonition and condemnation and short on invitation. Invitation is an act between and among equals. It is not arrogant, belittling, or self-righteous. It does not take the easy way of pointing to evil but does the harder, more challenging work of pointing to the good in the midst of evil. Invitation does not wallow in the stridency and anger of Jeremiah ("Woe to you, Jerusalem!") but finds reason to hope in the joy of Andrew ("Come and see the Lord"). Invitation does not water down the message but confronts the truth with honesty and integrity. Invitation does not deny the cross but embraces it with the conviction of Easter hope. Invitation is not a demand from a self-appointed expert or professional who believes he or she "possesses" some special insight to be given to lesser lights but a humble welcoming into the vineyard by a brother/sister pilgrim.

Which is *not* to say that invitation cannot be admonition. The gospel calls us to conversion and that means *change*—a change of attitude, a change of perspective, a change of approach—and change, as we all know too well, is difficult. Homilists should indeed address the call for conversion, but with the wisdom and compassion to understand that conversion demands difficult and sometimes radical change— and the humility to realize that such conversion is demanded of the homilist, as well. The homily should be an invitation to hope in the possibilities of such change and to embrace the grace of God that enables us to realize his kingdom of reconciliation and mercy in our broken, messy, incomplete lives.

On the practical, rhetorical level, a good closing should bring listeners back to the opening story. Referring back to the story you began with reinforces the unity (the "oneness") of the homily and focuses the audience's attention on the principal point of your homily.

Here's how the deacon ended the homily on the prodigal son and the stubborn husband:

> There are all kinds of mud puddles we find ourselves stuck in
> that we can't seem to pull ourselves out of.
> Let today's parable help us realize why and how we get stuck in that mud,
> why and how we find ourselves isolated in those pigsties,
> and are too proud or arrogant or selfish or greedy
>   to admit we've fallen into one;
> and let's promise ourselves, too,
> that we will never let our anger and hurt prevent us
> from pulling a loved one out of the mud—
> no matter how much he or she deserves to be left there.

And the homily on the "poor door" for the Solemnity of Christ the King ended with this invitation:

> May our prayer on this feast of Christ the King be
> that we might possess the humility and grace of the Lydias among us,
> to be able to see Jesus in everyone,
> so that we may be worthy enough—worthy enough ourselves—
> to one day enter God's dwelling place through the "poor door."

The *story/connection/invitation* model demands that homilists keep their antennae up and feelers out for the unmistakable signs of God's presence in the world that they share with their worshiping communities. Sometimes the gospel reading will trigger a story; at other times, a story, an event, or an image will come first, opening up in the homilist's imagination to a new dimension to a particular gospel account.

To preach as Jesus preached is, first and always, a matter of being in touch with the Word—the Word of God both made flesh in Jesus and fleshed out in the people of God and the world God gave them.

And that is what transforms preaching from a last-minute Saturday morning stress-filled burden into a weeklong ministry of service, in imitation of the preacher Jesus, who "opened his mouth in parables to proclaim what had been hidden from the foundation of the world" (see Matt 13:35).

Communicaré

Many preachers include some kind of story or "illustration" in their sermons—but often "bury" it in the middle of the homily. Take a look at a sermon you gave recently in which you used some kind of illustration, be it a story, an image, an anecdote, etc. Can you rewrite the sermon so that you *start* with that story?

Be on the lookout this week for a story in which you recognize the elements of a gospel story or event. The story may be something you see on television or read in a newspaper or discover in an online posting. Write out how you would connect that story to the gospel you have in mind.

Look at the ending of your last homily. How well did it express gospel "hope"? And did it refer back to your opening story (assuming you had one)? If not, can you rework the ending?

CHAPTER 7

You, the Proclaimer

To this point, the essays in this book have focused on the content of the homily: developing a homily that your audience can see, feel, and hear; a homily that serves as a mirror in which they see the Spirit of God moving in the loves and sorrows of their lives.

This chapter focuses on *you*: you the preacher and proclaimer. As such, you tell the story of God in your community's lived experience.

In other words, you are the channel of communications here.

Too often the emphasis on preaching has been on content (and, as admitted above, that has been the focus of this book thus far). Many a preacher will spend hours researching and writing his or her text; then, once the preacher determines the final text on paper is "it," the preacher is "ready."

The text may be "ready"—but is the preacher "ready"?

While the words express the idea, the homilist *embodies* it. The enthusiasm and conviction of a speaker have as much of an impact on an audience as the message itself. Everyone has heard a speaker who said all the right things but nobody believed them—the presenter's speaking mechanics were just not right, not in sync with the message.

The vocal and physical pieces of the homily have to be prepared in sync with the words. Though the text of the homily has been written, the homilist is only halfway there. If the homily were only a matter of coming up with the "right" combination of words, the homily could be duplicated in the parish bulletin or posted on the parish website, then on Sunday, read the gospel and then go right to the Creed.

The homilist's attitude and tone, both physically and vocally, make this presentation a homiletic *conversation*. The preacher's facial expressions and body language communicate as much hope as the gospel that is cited; the congregation reads as much from the presenter's posture as from the presentation itself. A congregation is moved by the homilist's confidence in the hope he or she is expressing; the credibility and integrity of the preacher's own living of the gospel has as great an impact on the congregation as the elegance of the words.

God speaks in every facet of your delivery. So, just as you have prepared the words of the homily, you have to prepare *yourself* to deliver these words. Preachers often gloss over this part of the preparation process. With so many demands on a minister's time, many homilists are relieved just to have the *words* on a piece of paper—the delivery they leave to the "Spirit" in the moment. Too many weekends, come Saturday evening, both the congregation and the homilist are hearing these words for the first time. And both are sometimes surprised at what they hear.

So this chapter challenges you to make time in the preaching process to sharpen the most critical tool you have in preaching: you.

Writing the Homily

Whether you preach from a manuscript or speak without notes or work off a sheet with a few key words, begin by writing the homily out *in full*. See all the words in front of you. Map out where you want to take the community. Know how long this journey is going to take.

Keep the sentences short and the structure simple: subject/verb/direct object. In everyday conversation, we don't speak in clauses and phrases— we speak in short verbal "spurts," fragments and one-word sentences. Remember that you are writing for the listener, not the reader.

As you write, follow the structure of story, connection, and invitation. Have that *one* point in front of you as you write.

Begin by writing out the opening story. Take the time to write that critical first sentence. Professional communicators know that a speaker has about seven seconds to "connect" with an audience, to make a positive impression, to convince his or her hearers that what you are about to say will be worth their time and attention.

Organize the story clearly and logically, so that the audience will be able to follow it. Include only the details that they will need to understand so that they can "see" the story unfold in their imagination.

Conclude the "story" section of your homily with a clear transition to the discussion part of the homily: how and why the story you have just told or the image you have just presented illustrates the point of the day's gospel. You might include other examples of where your listeners experience this gospel in their Monday-through-Saturday lives.

Be aware that every audience's attention span is limited. Whether a conference room of prospective clients, a seminar of undergraduates, or the congregation at Sunday's nine a.m. Mass, an audience is able to listen for only so long. So keep your focus on that *one* idea. Continue to give your listeners reasons to stay engaged.

Spend as much time and attention developing the ending of your homily. The most effective endings refer back to the opening story. The ending of the homily should make clear (again) that one, central idea you want the congregation to take home.

As you write your homily:

- Remember that the word *homily* means "conversation." Write as if you're talking to a friend. This is not a theological treatise or research paper; it is not a battle cry in the culture wars. Maintain an attitude of friendliness, compassion, and approachability. Don't talk above your hearers' heads—but don't talk down to them, either. You're walking the road to Emmaus together.

- Speaking in the first person can be very effective—but don't overdo it. Avoid the pronouns *I, me,* and *you* whenever you can. The homily is about *we* and *us.* The homily is neither for the glorification of the speaker nor an indictment of the congregation.

- Be careful of words and phrases that have become theological jargon: *grace, salvation, incarnation, redemption.* You may have a clear understanding of their meanings, but, for many of your listeners, these words and phrases are abstractions. Should you use such a word or phrase, explain what you mean and how your hearers experience that concept in their lives.

- Humor is not about telling jokes. It's about keeping it light, easy, nonjudgmental. A humorous touch is taking your message seriously—but not yourself. Remember this is about you, too: you are a fellow sinner and pilgrim with this community. So write like one.

- The thesaurus is a wonderful resource for finding the right, most exact word—not the most impressive word.

- Give yourself time to *rewrite*. Experienced writers know that good writing is a matter of correcting, changing, and editing, so they build time into every writing project to rewrite. Every writer has discovered that something that sounded so brilliant when he or she wrote it on Monday doesn't sound so insightful when read on Tuesday. It is far more constructive to spend one hour a day over several days to write a homily than trying to do it all—write, rewrite, and practice—in a single six-hour marathon on Saturday morning. As discussed below, few homilists ever take full possession of a Saturday morning rushed homily.

The Script

So you have a text.

Now you have to deliver it.

The first issue in prepping the preacher is the question of notes: What should you have in front of you at the ambo? One school of thought believes that preachers should not use any notes at all, that the preacher should be able to stand in the midst of the congregation and proclaim God's Word with confidence and conviction.

God bless you if you can.

And there are, to be sure, some preachers who can do that most effectively. But few homilists are able to do that the first time they preach. That kind of confidence develops with experience. The "upside" of this approach, of course, is that without notes the preacher's full attention is on the audience, that there is a real sense of *conversation* between preacher and congregation.

But there is a downside. In the course of preaching, the temptation to go off on a tangent can be too great, that a sudden burst of inspiration can take the homily in a direction that may derail the focus or main point of the homily. Inexperienced homilists, working without a "safety net" of written notes, can easily lose their train of thought and struggle to get the train back on track.

If working without notes is something you aspire to, start small. Begin in small venues, such as at weekday liturgies, and speak for a minute or two, maybe with a few key words on a piece of paper to keep you on track. Over time, as your skills develop and your confidence grows, try longer presentations before larger groups (reflections for retreats or meditations for parish organizations). You'll know when to make the leap to the Sunday homily.

Preaching without notes and *memorizing* the homily are not the same things. Memorizing is to commit to a specific set and order of words. The goal is to articulate the text exactly as written. Memorization is actually more confining than speaking from notes: the preacher who has memorized his or her homily is more concerned about getting the words out than with making a connection with the audience. So don't try to memorize the homily—unless you're an experienced, skilled actor, your presentation will sound mechanical and passionless, failing to engage your hearers.

The other end of the spectrum is preaching with a complete manuscript. Speech communication books like this one typically advise homilists not to bring a complete manuscript with them to the ambo. But the fact is there are some very good homilists who do use a complete manuscript for the Sunday homily—and they know how to make it work. Others use very detailed notes at the ambo. With a fully written script, the focus and unity of the homily remains intact; the preacher keeps control of the message and the timing.

But most inexperienced homilists who bring a complete manuscript with them to the ambo usually fall into the trap of reading it—and it *sounds* read and artificial to the audience, who quickly disengage from the conversation.

You have to discover for yourself what works best for you. With experience, you will realize what you need to make yourself both comfortable and comforting in your preaching. Every audience immediately picks up whether a speaker is at ease with the role of preacher or if the preacher is struggling. If a presenter has demonstrated that he or she cares, if a speaker is inviting and engaging, audiences will stay with the speaker even when he or she needs a moment to find his or her place or when grappling to come up with a word or when backing up to clarify what he or she struggled to express—provided they believe the speaker has something to say that will be of benefit to them. But audiences will distance themselves from the speaker who doesn't seem happy to be speaking to them or who sees this presentation as beneath (or above) them. Audiences will not engage a speaker whose attitude and message do not engage them. And audiences will not forgive the speaker who is unprepared.

So, like every effective speaker, homilists need to "prep" before Sunday—or, to be blunt, *rehearse*.

Whether you work with a full script or a handful of notes, you have to *know* the homily. You have to be aware of how the homily progresses, how it moves forward, how it sounds. When you go from page 2 to page 3, nothing on the new page should surprise you.

Start by setting up your rehearsal script in "sense" lines. Note that in the sample homilies that appear throughout this book, the sentences have not run on until a new paragraph; each line of text ends at a natural breaking point when read aloud (the Lectionary currently in use breaks the Scripture texts down into such "sense lines" for lectors). Anticipating where you will break, pause, and breathe is an important step in coming to *know* the homily.

Once you have your notes together, practice delivering the homily *out loud*. That cannot be stressed enough—practice out loud, using the "voice" you will use on Sunday. Going over the text "in your head" or mumbling it quietly accomplishes little. You have to make your brain and voice work together to bring your homily to life. Rehearse the homily out loud as many times as it takes to get it down—especially the details of the story, the transitions from point to point, and the closing. You will hear immediately that some words that look terrific on paper do not "sound" so terrific when you say them out loud. You will realize more precise words and phrases that sound more natural and clearer. You will find places needing editing. You will discover how to improve the flow and rhythm of the presentation. You will also get a sense of timing, of where you should pause, of which words need to be hit harder or softer or slower (more on the voice and body below). You will realize the clutter of words and preponderance of ideas that will lose your hearers and distract them from grasping your original *one* idea.

Rehearse your homily out loud several times, over two or three days, if you can. (Again, better to rehearse a few minutes a day than in one long session at the last minute.)

Once you think you have it down, put the outline aside and try giving it again out loud. Yes, you're going to stumble, lose your place, and, at some point, come to a dead stop. But it will help you better learn the flow of the homily and identify where the difficult transitions are.

The more you come to *know* your material, the more the homily will become *yours*: the more comfortable and at ease you will be (which will translate to the audience), the more poise and confidence you will possess as you preach, the more natural your gestures and physical punctuations will be.

It is also important to get used to your notes or script: how the words are laid out on the page. As you rehearse with your notes, you may find that slipping one page out of the way and going to the next comes at an awkward point, so you will want to rewrite your notes so that you end a page at the end of a complete idea and start the next page at a natural transition point. Some speakers use only half or three-quarters of a side of paper in writing out their text so as not to lower their eyes too far down as they speak and thus risk losing eye contact with their audience. You will also find that a certain font size and line spacing is easier for you to see; you'll also develop your own system of symbols (underlining, circling, etc.) to help you emphasize key words and phrases.

An important part of the rehearsal process is to get used to working with your notes, sliding them out of the way with a minimal amount of distraction and learning where and how to find your place on your script again each time you look down after making eye contact with your audience.

Two other suggestions from the professionals: Don't staple your pages together and don't speak from a "stack" of small index cards. Have everything in front of you on three or four sides of 8-1/2 x 11-inch paper. Keep the paper shuffling to a minimum. The constant flipping of pages and shuffling of cards is a preventable distraction.

The goal of all this is to take possession of these words. You have to make these words your own. And that requires taking the time to rehearse—*standing up and out loud.*

Finding Your Voice

As well as getting to know the text, rehearsing the homily is a matter of discovering how to use your voice and body to deliver the message. The human voice possesses a number of abilities that can express meaning to a message more effectively than words themselves:

Tone: The tone of your voice expresses your passion, your empathy, your caring, far more effectively and believably than your saying "I care about this" or "I'm committed to this." In the tone of your voice, an audience also hears that "edge" of anger, exhaustion, or arrogance that you may be trying to hide. The tone of your voice will always give you away. But positive emotions—joy, excitement, and sincerity—are also revealed in the tone of your voice. Regardless of the words they are hearing, listeners will detect the homilist's true feelings and attitudes in the tone of the speaker's voice.

Inflection: How you say a word—the emphasis you place on it when you say it, the rising and lowering of your voice when you express it, the hardness in your articulating the word or your softness when you utter it—expresses the importance you are placing on it. *Inflection* is the human voice's ability to emphasize, accent, or "attack" a word in such a way as to give it new and precise meanings, without the use of additional adjectives or adverbs or explanations. Even simple words like *yes, no,* and *please* can be given entirely new and different meanings, depending on how a speaker emphasizes the word.

Pitch: Related to inflection is pitch: the highness and lowness of one's voice. Generally speaking, a higher pitch indicates excitement or urgency, while a lower pitch creates a sense of solemnity or seriousness. As the voice rises in pitch, it tends to carry better through a room than a lower-pitched voice; lower-pitched voices can easily become muffled, throaty, or breathy and, consequently, be more difficult to hear and understand. But voices that become too high in pitch can grate on listeners (the "screeching chalk on the blackboard" effect). Just about every speaker can adjust the pitch of his or her voice, so a speaker with a naturally higher-pitched voice can, with effort and practice, lower his or her pitch.

Pace: Slowing down to express an idea or picking up the pace can serve as an oral highlighter; pausing and even stopping give the audience time to take in what you have said, to see in their imaginations the image you have presented. A quickened speaking rate can indicate excitement, urgency, and enthusiasm, while a slower speaking rate not only adds emphasis but makes the details of an important point easier for the audience to grasp and follow.

Pausing: Sometimes the most effective speaking device is . . . not speaking. A well-timed pause gives the listeners time to "absorb" what you have just said, giving them the opportunity to create their own images to accompany your words, thereby increasing retention (and preventing information overload). Stopping for a moment commands attention to what you have said or are about to say. In relating a story or before making a key point, a strategically placed pause creates the element of suspense. Pausing works to the speaker's advantage, as well: stopping helps the speaker eliminate the "non-words" and nervous distractions. Inexperienced speakers believe that they have to keep the show moving, so they fill what would otherwise be empty air with annoying non-words like "um" and "er" and meaningless verbiage like "okay" and "really." The more experience speakers gain before audiences, the more comfortable and confident they become with pausing.

The human voice also possesses a number of other properties that can enhance a speaker's message. A basic but critical property of the human voice is *articulation*, the physical ability to make the sounds that the audience will recognize as words. *Pronunciation* is the correct way to pronounce a word ("nuclear" instead of "new-cu-lar"); enunciation is the clarity with which a speaker actually says those correctly pronounced words (examples of poor enunciation: "guvment" for government, "gonna" for going to, and "singin'" for singing).

Very few homilists and public speakers speak too slowly; most have a tendency to speak too fast. A homilist whose delivery seems too slow may often have a greater problem: a monotone voice so devoid of variations in pitch and inflection that the community quickly loses interest in what he or she is saying.

A problem for some speakers is dropping the sounds of the last consonants of words or syllables. Not only does such mumbling sound sloppy (see enunciation, above), but it can make it very difficult for the listener to hear what the speaker is saying—especially if the sentence contains a string of words with similar sounding vowels and consonants. The only effective solution is to enunciate last consonant sounds carefully and deliberately, as distinctly as you can, even if you think that you are exaggerating the sounds to the point of sounding foolish. Rest assured that it will not sound foolish or exaggerated to the listeners in the last rows of the church or hall.

Finally, be aware of falling into a predictable, sing-song rhythm. Nervousness can put a speaker on automatic pilot and a speech takes on a constant, unchanging speech pattern. At one end of the spectrum is the monotone that does not change inflection or speaking rate at all; at the other end is the equally annoying "false interrogative": the raising of the voice at the end of every sentence, turning every statement into a question. This tendency—which first-time speakers are often completely unaware of—projects uncertainty and can be perceived as "talking down" to the audience.

Stand and Deliver

As you get your voice into the text, your body becomes more engaged as well. Your physical presence and attitude also communicate in ways that can affect the reception of your message:

Eye contact: The eyes create a bond between the speaker and the listener: direct eye contact is perceived as sincere, earnest, forthright, and confident. Due primarily to television, all audiences have come to expect direct eye contact from every speaker, whether priest or politician. Eye contact begins by seeing the congregation or audience not as some amorphous mass of humanity but as individual human beings. Many inexperienced homilists and speakers are too willing to sacrifice eye contact for the "smooth" recitation of their words. They believe that reading the text of their presentation, word for word, is better than stumbling and tripping over their words. But most audiences will gladly tolerate a few jerky starts and stops on the part of the speaker if they sense that the presenter is working to connect with them, that the homilist is attempting to talk with them and not "at" them. That bond is established, first, in a speaker's eye contact with the audience.

Smiling: Walk into a room full of people, especially people you do not know. Who are the individuals you find yourself gravitating toward? Those who smile. A smile is the major bridge-builder in communications: a smile allays fears, invites and welcomes others to "come on over," and establishes bonds of friendship and trust. Even the most solemn of liturgies is not undermined by a smile of welcome and invitation. And smiling is as much an attitude and a way of thinking as it is a physical movement. Photographers will tell you that we smile as much with our eye muscles as with our mouths. In other words, *think* smile.

Gestures: Well-timed and natural gestures also add impact to a point. *Conventional gestures* are signs and symbols that everyone understands, such as numbers or a raised palm indicating "Stop!" *Descriptive gestures* indicate size or direction. Some verbs can be described in gestures: washing, for example, can be indicated with the hand wiping clean an imaginary blackboard. And gestures can serve as *markers* or *indicators* that punctuate or emphasize ideas, such as a clenched fist for anger or solidarity, cupped or clasped hands symbolizing community or completeness, an extended hand inviting the audience to join an effort. Gestures work only when they are *natural*: the key is to be relaxed and comfortable, letting the gestures happen. Gestures do not work if they are forced or half-hearted.

Posture: Good posture projects authority and integrity and reinforces your enthusiasm for your topic and for the audience. Maintaining good posture is simple: just keep both feet flat on the floor. Standing stiffly and motionless when addressing the congregation is not natural. The speaker who stands rigidly, regardless of the words uttered, is communicating either "I am scared to death of all of you" or "I am vastly superior to all of you."

The speaker who is careless in maintaining his or her posture (slumping over or leaning on the podium, for example) is telling the audience, "I really don't want to do this" or "I'm too 'cool' to be here—speaking to you now is a waste of my time." But, again, body movement and gesturing cannot be forced; the more a homilist becomes comfortable at the lectern, the more he or she develops the confidence to let the body become a natural part of preaching and presenting.

Animated movement is one thing, but nervous twitching, pacing, and shaking—or what an audience perceives as such—is entirely different. What the speaker might intend as enthusiastic engagement might be perceived by the audience as nervous energy, making everyone in the audience uneasy. What the speaker may think is a cool, professional exterior may, in fact, be read by the audience as aloofness and cold dispassion toward the subject or the congregation, or simply annoying and distracting.

When is something distracting? When the audience starts wondering or whispering, "I wish he'd stop wandering around the church."

Remember, too, that the lectern is there not as a defense mechanism or as a brace to hold you up. The lectern or ambo is a piece of furniture designed for function, the function of holding the notes and materials you need for your homily. Use it for that purpose—or not at all.

Most homilists and speakers experience some form of nervousness before a presentation. That is as it should be—in fact, nervousness is a positive sensation that prevents the homilist from oversimplifying the task and serves as a control mechanism: stopping the presenter from doing or saying something "ill advised." Think of nervousness as a kind of "safety valve."

Nervousness is a physical as well as a mental (or spiritual) phenomenon. Notice that when you are nervous, your pulse rate increases rapidly. With the blood surging through your body, your breathing becomes quick and short. So, when you are nervous, take a deep breath, not from the upper ribs, but from the "gut"—that is, from the diaphragm, the large muscle that moves up and down between the abdominal and thoracic cavities. Exhale all the air out of your lungs so that your shoulders shrug. Now inhale, deeply and slowly; then let the air out again, slowly. Take a few long breaths and then try to project your voice clearly and loudly. You will find that you have greater voice control and power. You may still be anxious, but you should have a new sense of energy and dynamism in your voice.

Your nervousness will always find some outlet: for some speakers, nervousness will cause them to pace; others will ceaselessly tap their fingers on the edge of the podium, twitch, constantly shuffle their notes, or race through their speech. And most will not even realize they are doing these things. Be aware of how your nervousness manifests itself and then rechannel that energy into the dynamics of your homily.

And take to heart the advice of a wise college professor of rhetoric to a student almost debilitated by nervousness: "Imagine the absolute worst possible thing that could happen. Then remember that it won't."

All of these vocal and physical dimensions can communicate a great deal in any speech or homily—but none of these dynamics are possible unless you employ them. And that takes preparation. So start your homily prep by getting your tongue and palate around the words you have written—and realize that you are going to be changing them. Get your voice into the rhythm of the story, the flow of ideas, the building up to the conclusion and exit line. As you work with these words out loud, you'll discover what sounds true and what comes across as forced, unconvincing, or false. You'll stumble over the clunky phrases and the needlessly cumbersome exposition. You'll finally "hear" how this conversation should develop and rewrite and edit and change accordingly.

Once the words become yours, write up the notes you need or lay out the script to keep you on track. As you preach more and more, you may find yourself needing fewer and fewer notes at the ambo. Whether you use a handful of key words or several complete sentences is not the issue: what is important is that you realize what you need to deliver this homily that comes from your heart and soul—and brain.

Pulpit Notes: **The Christmas Truce of World War I**

The compelling 2005 French film *Joyeux Noel* inspired this Christmas 2015 homily. Its construction demonstrates some of the concepts discussed above in terms of writing the homily and rehearsing the delivery.

This is the actual text the homilist had at the ambo. As well as being broken into "sense lines," included are some of the markings the preacher added to the text to help his delivery.

First, the story.

One hundred and one Christmases ago tonight—
Christmas Eve, 1914:
World War I had been underway for five months
and would continue for another <u>three-and-a-half bloody years</u>.
The first modern technological war:
the first time that <u>tanks</u>, <u>machine guns</u>, <u>poison gas</u>, and <u>airplanes</u> were used
    in battle.
All horribly efficient.

But on Christmas Eve 1914, something remarkable takes place:
a spontaneous cease-fire.
All sides lay down their weapons to observe the birth of the Savior—
the Savior all combatants believed was on *their* side.

In the first draft of this homily, this is how the above read:

World War I was the bloodiest conflict the world had ever seen. It was the first war in which such technological advances as tanks, machine guns, poison gas, and airplanes were used. It all proved to be horribly efficient. On Christmas Eve—101 years ago tonight—in the fifth month into this bloody conflict, something extraordinary happened: a cease-fire.

But as the homilist began working with the text, he realized that the phrase "101 Christmases ago" made a powerful connection with the present. And so that phrase became the first words of the homily—and will be repeated at the end.

As he rehearsed the text, the homilist found himself not speaking in complete sentences, but in simple phrases, each punctuated by pauses. As he continued his preparation work, he underlined key words so that he would see them as such in his text. Notice, for example, that the phrase *three-and-a-half bloody years* is underscored with a single, unbroken line—to remind the homilist that this phrase needs to be said as if it was a single word in order to accurately convey its meaning.

The homilist continued the story.

The beautiful 2005 French film *Joyeux Noel* recounts one story of the World
   War I Christmas truce:
Three regiments—one French, one Scottish, and one German—
are literally dug into a French field.
For weeks, each side has been trying to annihilate the other from their dirty,
   cold trenches.
Then, on Christmas Eve, the fighting suddenly stops.
All weapons and artillery are stilled.
No cannon barrages set fire to the sky.
All is quiet.

In the Germans' foxhole,
a soldier—a renowned opera singer—
begins to sing "Silent Night" for his comrades.
From the other side of the field,
Scottish bagpipers pick up the melody and play along.
Then the pipers begin to play *Adeste Fideles*,
   and the German tenor sings along with them.
Soon soldiers from each side peer over <u>no-man's-land</u>
   and cautiously climb over the trenches
   and meet in the middle of the frozen farmland.
They offer Christmas greetings—
   and despite their different languages, the meaning comes across.
Their dirty, grim faces begin to break into smiles.

Soon they're exchanging photographs of wives and children and girlfriends
and sharing their precious parcels of chocolate and wine,
of sausages, and tins of cookies and cakes sent from home.

The priest from the Scottish regiment offers Mass in the cold field
and the combatants kneel and pray together.

Note that the homilist is speaking in the present tense here, as if the
movie is being screened for the congregation. The first draft of the
homily was written in the past tense—but, as he worked with the text,
the preacher found himself naturally relating the story in the present
tense. The present tense can be an effective way for engaging an audience in any story.

On Christmas morning,
French, Scot, and German help one another bury their dead comrades,
    whose bodies have been rotting in the frozen snow and barbed wire of
        the battlefield.
The goodwill extends into Christmas afternoon,
    as the soldiers happily skirmish in a soccer game.

Then, at nightfall on December 25, the war resumes.

Here the homilist pauses before the next line:

But not on that field in France.

He pauses again before continuing:

Because the men in those other foxholes are not enemies anymore.
They're no longer anonymous soldiers fighting under an alien flag.
They're fellow <u>fathers and sons and brothers</u>.
They're <u>farmers and masons and bakers and artists and clerks</u>.
They now have names; they now have histories.
Christmas has transformed them into brothers.

Note the use of the contraction *They're* for *They are*. That's how people naturally talk in a conversation. Contractions are used throughout the text.

When the general staffs of the three armies discover what has happened,
the officers of the three regiments are severely reprimanded
and the soldiers are punished for fraternizing with the enemy.
The French and Scottish units are disbanded;
the Germans are sent to the eastern front to fight the Russians.

There's a brief pause here as an introduction to the next part of the story:

And the Scottish priest who celebrated the Christmas Eve Mass
is ordered by his bishop to return to his parish in Scotland immediately.
The priest pleads to remain with the troops,
but the bishop will not hear of it.
Before launching into a haughty <u>God-is-on-our-side</u> sermon for new recruits,

the bishop angrily admonishes the priest:

"May our Lord Jesus Christ guide your steps back to the <u>straight and narrow</u>
    path."

But the devastated priest asks, "Is that truly the path of the Lord?"

The preacher tries to capture the restrained outrage of the bishop
(played by British actor Ian Richardson in the film):

The bishop coldly replies, "You're *not* asking the *right* questions."

The bishop's admonition serves as the ideal transition point, connecting the story to the point of the Christmas gospel:

But that <u>is</u> the point.
The coming of Christ <u>changes</u> the questions.
In Christ, it's no longer about me—it's about <u>us</u>.
In Christ, it's not <u>my</u> wants and satisfaction that matter—
    it's the <u>common good</u> that matters.
In Christ, it's not about avenging old hatreds that divide us—
    it's about building a new world <u>on what unites</u> all of us.
In Christ, it's not about merely avoiding confrontation—
    it's about doing the hard, hard work of making peace.

In the first draft, the phrase "In Christ" only appeared once, at the
beginning of the list: "In Christ, it's no longer about me—it's about <u>us</u>."

But as the homilist practiced the piece out loud, he found himself
repeating the phrase at the beginning of each "question." The repetition of "In Christ" is a form of *anaphora*, the repeating of a key word
or phrase that effectively underscores each point and makes it more
memorable to the audience.

The questions are written in the same parallel structure—"it's not
about . . . it's about . . ."—another rhetorical device called *parallelism*
that makes a point more memorable and visual to the hearer.

The theme of this homily is that the coming of Christ changes the
way we see our world and one another. The homilist continues this
theme with two more images:

Christmas is not just a cease-fire on our busy calendars—
Christmas is a <u>sea change</u>

in which God re-creates our humanity in his love—
a love that becomes real in the Child born in a Palestinian cave.

On this night, the <u>light</u> that is of God <u>first dawns</u>:
the light of God's compassion and mercy
that changes our perspective of the world—and of one another,
enabling us to see everyone and everything as God sees it.
Christmas changes <u>us</u> and how <u>we see the world</u>
    and how <u>we see one another</u>.

The conclusion of the homily went through several drafts—each time becoming simpler and clearer. The final version is the following: a simple series of examples drawn from the film and Luke's narrative that apply to the everyday experience of the congregation—and including the opening words of the homily, "One hundred and one Christmases ago":

Oh, we're a long, long way from realizing
    God's vision of peace on earth to all people of goodwill.
But we <u>can</u> bring the peace of Christmas into our own
    <u>battlefields and bunkers</u>.
We <u>can</u> open our <u>mangers and inns</u> to welcome the Christ Child.
We <u>can</u> give birth to God's beloved in our <u>homes and hearts</u>.
We <u>can</u> reflect the light that first dawns at Christmas:
    the light that shines through time
        to transform a bloody battlefield in France <u>101 Christmases ago</u>,
    the light that now illuminates our broken world
        on this Christmas, 2015.

Once the homilist decided to center the homily on the story of the Christmas truce, the text went through several drafts. He spent a few minutes each evening for a full week before Christmas rehearsing out loud, tweaking and rewriting it along the way as he came to know the homily, to hear it, to see it. And as he came to get his voice and body into the movement of the story, connection, and closing, the homily became *his*. He could engage the audience in a conversation about the Christmas story as part of their stories.

Communicaré

Take a famous speech or poem and prepare it for delivery. For example, think about how Lincoln might sound delivering his second inaugural address; imagine the old Persian mystic recounting the story of his journey many years before to seek out the infant King in T. S. Eliot's poem "The Journey of the Magi"; or listen to the old Vermont farmer relate, in such a chilling, matter-of-fact voice, the horrible accident that takes place in the Robert Frost poem "Out, Out—." Read these works out loud: break the text down so that you are able to capture the nuances, the rhythm, the voice of the speaker. Despite the formality of some of the language, see if you can deliver these pieces as if they were conversations with the audience/readers.

Reading poetry aloud or speeches from plays and movies is a great exercise to sharpen the vocal skills of both the first-time preacher and the experienced presenter. You might also try reading *aloud* the psalms of the Liturgy of the Hours—you'll begin to "see" and "hear" the beautiful imagery in these prayers, as well as develop your vocal skills.

Every homilist recalls a homily that just didn't "sound right." Pull yours out and work it through again, employing the vocal skills discussed above. Note the ways you can make it sound "clearer" through editing and clarifying the text itself and sharpening your vocal articulation of the text.

CHAPTER 8

You, the Minister

In July 1838, the faculty of the Divinity College at Harvard invited alumnus Ralph Waldo Emerson to address the students.

The speech was not well received.

Emerson had left the ministry a few years before—the death of his young wife drove him to question both his beliefs and profession. Emerson's Divinity College remarks challenged what he saw as a lifeless Christian tradition and religion's inability to encounter God in the hearts of every man and woman. The Harvard address was a watershed moment in the American Transcendental movement.

Emerson's controversial address that evening included this portrait:

> I once heard a preacher who sorely tempted me to say I would go to church no more. . . . A snow-storm was falling around us. The snow-storm was real, the preacher merely spectral, and the eye felt the sad contrast in looking at him, and then out of the window behind him into the beautiful meteor of the snow. He had lived in vain. He had no one word intimating that he had laughed or wept, was married or in love, had been commended, or cheated, or chagrined. If he had ever lived or acted, we were none the wiser for it. The capital secret of his profession, namely, *to convert life into truth,* he had not learned. Not one fact in all his experience had he yet imported into his doctrine. This man had ploughed and planted and talked and bought and sold; he had read books; he had eaten and drunken; his head aches, his heart throbs; he smiles and suffers; and yet there was not a surmise, a hint, in all the discourse that he had ever lived

at all. Not a line did he draw out of real history. The true preacher can be known by this, that he deals out to the people his life,—*life passed through the fire of thought.*[1]

Life passed through the fire of thought: an insightful definition of the preaching ministry not only for a nineteenth-century New England village pastor but for those who preach to twenty-first-century parish communities as well.

The previous chapter focused on the preacher as communicator, as the vehicle for proclaiming the Sunday homily. This final essay reflects on the preacher as minister. The ministry of preaching, as Emerson realizes on a cold New England Sunday morning, does not begin at the ambo or pulpit. Preaching is the product of the preacher's lived experience. What makes the preacher a faithful spouse, a loving parent, a trusted friend, a conscientious worker also makes him or her a good preacher. The ministry of proclaiming the Word of God not only takes place at the lectern, but also at the bedside, in the funeral home, in the classroom, around a conference or seminar table, in someone's living room. To preach well and effectively is a mindset; it requires keeping one's eyes and ears—and soul—open to the presence of the always present, if often hidden, God. The work of "enfleshing" the Word of God begins and ends with experiencing what Emerson calls *life passed through the fire of thought.*

"Life"

Faithful preaching is about life: life in all its joys and victories, life in all its messiness and confusion, life in all its missteps and disappointments. The preacher is not just a detached observer of life, but a full participant in life. It is life that the preacher shares with every member of the congregation.

From the first Christian assemblies, the Sunday homily was envisioned to be grounded in the Monday-through-Saturday life of the community. It is to point to the presence of God in the midst of our "ploughing" and planting, our laughing and crying, our headaches and heart breaks. As Christ reveals to us a God who is the loving Father of his children, the preacher is called to reveal that same God who comforts, consoles, illuminates, and animates our lives.

The "secret" of effective preaching, Emerson believed, is in revealing the truth of God's compassion and forgiveness in the generosity, kindness, and commitment of the saints who live in our midst. The Word we proclaim cannot stand apart and aloof from the "landscape" but be grounded in the very midst of it.

The Sunday Word should also be spoken in the *language* of life. Just as Jesus preached in parables about lost sheep, wayward children, and germinating seeds, contemporary preachers are most effective in telling stories of the holy and sacred in their communities—stories about juggling school and sports schedules, making one's way through life's moral quagmires, working through ethical conundrums that were unimaginable just a generation ago.

We church folk often sound like we want people to abandon their lives and embrace God's grace in a different existence, in a safe bubble detached from the evil of the world. But as John the Baptizer proclaims in the Fourth Gospel, the Lamb of God walks among us. Our challenge as a church is to reveal the love of God in our midst: God in our own Nazareths and Galilees, God at table with us in our own mortgaged cenacles, God bearing our crosses with us.

As Teresa of Avila counseled her sisters, "God moves among the pots and pans."

Certainly deacons bring a special insight into the ministry of proclaiming the Word. Most have families and careers. They live their lives in the "landscape" of the neighborhood and community, the workplace and marketplace. Part of the deacon's call is to realize the presence of God and the demands of discipleship in the many "Godless" places where we live our lives. From that realization should come the stories the deacon tells on Sundays.

"Fire"

The image of "fire" evokes power, energy, and purification. In Christian imagery, fire is the symbol of the Spirit of God animating and illuminating the community of the baptized.

We are a church that has been purified and perfected in the Pentecost "fire" of the Spirit of God—the *ruah* of God's love, justice, and forgiveness. The fire of that Spirit illuminates the road we travel to God's dwelling place, melts away the coldness of sin that isolates us from God and from one another, and empowers us to realize our baptismal call to become prophets of God and disciples of his Christ.

That is the fire that Emerson speaks of, the fire of the Gospel of Jesus: the limitless and unconditional love of God that continues to create and re-create in our own time and place. God's love can be a vehicle for transformation, a balm for healing, an agent for gathering together the lost and forgotten. It is the preacher's call to help his or her community realize such possibilities in their own time and place.

The community has to sense that "fire" within the deacon/preacher. But that "fire" is not a matter of projecting a persona or spirituality. That "fire" is not kindled only in the clever phrase, entertaining story, or flawless delivery.

That fire Emerson saw is experienced in trust and humility.

At ordination, the deacon is entrusted with certain responsibilities and tasks for the good of the church. It is the charism of trust, not "power." And, in the sacrament of holy orders, the church is saying to the people of God, "You can trust this guy. We've checked him out. We've done due diligence. He's studied and prayed and comes at this with the right attitude and heart. And you have to hold him account-able. Remind him that this is *not* about him, but *us.*"

At your diaconal ordination, you were entrusted with proclaiming the Word. And you proclaim that Word, first, in the happiness of your own life and your generosity of spirit and kindness of heart. That happiness and generosity will be perceived by your hearers in every word you speak in your ministry, whether from the ambo or over a cup of coffee. "Receive the Gospel of Christ, whose herald you now are. Believe what you read, teach what you believe, and practice what you teach," the bishop said to you as he presented you with the Book of the Gospels at ordination.[2]

Humility is also a flame of this "fire." But humility is much more than taking the last place; it is not a call to disappear into the background. Humility is centered in the realization that every human being is a son or daughter of God. The English word *humility* comes from the Latin word for soil, *humus.* Like the rich, broken soil of humus, humility is the capacity to be open to receiving the seeds of experience—both the painful and the enriching—in order to grow in wisdom and understanding. Humility is the grace to let ourselves be "broken" —broken of our pride, our ego, our wants—in order to realize a harvest far greater than ourselves, a harvest that is possible only through gener-ous openness, selfless giving, and enlightened gratitude. Humility is to recognize and lift up the gifts of everyone, gifts as valuable as our own and deserving to be of service to the common good. "Humble" ministry enables others to find purpose and meaning in using their gifts and abilities for the good of all.

The spirituality of the deacon/preacher should be centered in such humility: humility that begins with valuing life as a gift from God, a gift we have received only through God's mysterious love, not through anything we have done to deserve it. In faith that begins with such spiritual "humus": we can bring forth love from barrenness, we can find reason to hope in the midst of despair, we can see the light that enables us to make our way out of the darkest places.

Trust that leads to joyful servanthood, humility that enables one to lift up and heal—the fire of the ministry of preaching.

"Thought"

Emerson laments that the preacher on that snowy Sunday speaks from a series of ethical and moral principles that remain vague and remote; the poor man seems intent on keeping the Gospel at arm's length from life, including the preacher's own.

Preaching that is of God comes out of a preacher's own journey, a preacher's own searching for the holy in his or her life, a preacher's coping with his or her own doubts and disappointments. Preaching begins in the wilderness of the heart, with Christ as one's desert companion. Make no mistake: It is a difficult journey. It requires us to let go of the "beliefs" and values we find most comforting and dare to walk where God's love seems hidden and alien. It compels us to refocus our vision of God from the "likeness" that we have created of God to the "image" in which God created us. It forces us to free God from the limits we have set on God, to allow God to rise up out of the tombs in which we have buried him, and realize that God's grace and love are far greater in breadth and scope than we imagine.

Such "thought" begins in the prayer of "mulling" over the gospel. Emerson's ideal of faithful preacher has his or her eyes open and senses attuned to the presence of God in and around the community the preacher is called to serve.

The deacon/preacher, then, must be a person of prayer—and not just the formal, ritualized prayer of the church. He must find his own "out of the way" place and let God do the talking in the depths of his heart.

He must make time to step back and discern the Spirit of God in his midst—not because he has to stand up and preach but because he seeks to live that Spirit. He has to love first before he can preach about love; he has to know God before he can reveal him; he has to realize his own pain and shortcomings before he dare speak a word of healing and peace.

To possess the heart and mind of Jesus begins with embracing his model of being a servant to others. So, in reality, everyone in the church is a deacon (as well as "priest, prophet and king"); in baptism, everyone is called to serve and love one another as Jesus did. That's Christ's vision of church—and it is that vision that the deacon/preacher is called to proclaim.

So, if you're serious about preaching, you need to find your mountain or desert to ponder your own questions and doubts, to find that shard of light that is the grace of God illuminating your next step.

Life passed through the fire of thought.

May Emerson's vision of preaching be realized in our own village churches: the Word of God proclaimed in the midst of our snowstorms and not apart from them, the Word uncovered and lifted up in life in all its glorious messiness, the Word living in our midst in the smallest acts of compassion, justice, and peace.

Communicaré

In what situations and venues—other than Mass—have you found yourself "preaching"? How might you better prepare yourself for those situations?

Do you ever find yourself feeling like the "spectral" preacher described by Emerson? Has a homily you preached failed to "convert life into truth"? How would you approach that homily differently?

Review your entire process of preaching—from your first reading of the text to your delivery of the homily on Sunday. Are you giving yourself sufficient time just to ponder and pray over the text? Are you rushing through or shortchanging the time you need to prepare yourself to deliver the homily, to "know" the homily you are going to preach?

Consider forming a "preachers' support group" with two or three fellow preachers. You might meet every few weeks and read and pray together the gospels to be read on the Sundays ahead and spend some time on the "four questions" asked earlier in this book:

- What is the single most striking word, sentence, or image in this gospel?

- Where and how do we see this gospel in our time and place?

- What is Jesus asking us to do?

- How does this gospel reveal God's love in our midst?

Is there someone who might serve as your "mentor" in preaching? Not necessarily another priest or deacon, your "mentor" should be someone whose judgment you trust, whose opinion you value, who will give you a supportive but honest evaluation of your homilies. A good mentor will point out specific ways you might improve your delivery and suggest, from his or her life and experience, new and fresh insights into a gospel text.

Notes

Chapter 1

1. This material has been adapted with permission from Massachusetts Eye and Ear who holds the copyright thereto.

Chapter 2

1. M. Craig Barnes, *The Pastor as Minor Poet: Texts and Subtexts in the Ministerial Life* (Grand Rapids, MI: Eerdmans, 2009), 35–36.

2. Thomas Reese, "Pope Francis says no to boring homilies," *National Catholic Reporter* (April 30, 2015).

3. Joel Stein, "The New Greatest Generation: Why Millennials Will Save Us All," *Time* (May 20, 2013).

4. Rachel Held Evans, "Want millennials back in the pews? Stop trying to make church 'cool,'" *The Washington Post* (April 30, 2015).

Chapter 3

1. Walter J. Burghardt, *Preaching: The Art and the Craft* (Mahwah, NJ: Paulist Press, 1987), 14.

2. Lauren F. Winner, "Interrupted," Living by the Word, *The Christian Century* 25, no. 25 (December 16, 2008): 20.

3. Anne Lamott, *Traveling Mercies: Some Thoughts on Faith* (New York: Pantheon Books, 1999), 100, 101.

4. Adapted from Glennon Doyle Melton, "Share This with All the Schools, Please," momastery.com, January 30, 2014, http://momastery.com/blog/2014/01/30/share-schools/.

5. Steve Coogan and Jeff Pope, *Philomena*, directed by Stephen Frears (The Weinstein Company, 2013). Based on the book *The Lost Child of Philomena Lee* by Martin Sixsmith.

6. David Von Drehle, with Jay Newton-Small and Maya Rhodan, "Murder, Race and Mercy: Stories from Charleston," *Time* (November 23, 2015): 50.

7. Jeffrey Collins, "Families of Charleston victims offer forgiveness," Associated Press (June 20, 2015).

8. Daniel J. Harrington, "Lectio Divina," *America* (March 31, 2003).

Chapter 4

1. *Advertising Age*, October 8, 2013.

2. John J. Conley, "How Not to Preach," Philosopher's Notebook, *America* (February 2, 2015).

Chapter 5

1. Anthony J. Zavagnin, "Lessons of the Heart: My first days as a father in the I.C.U.," Faith in Focus, *America* (June 8–15, 2015).

Chapter 6

1. Bill McNabb, "Garrison Keillor: Off the Air," *The Door* (January/February 1996).

2. Heidi Neumark, "The Poor Door: Class separation in the church," *The Christian Century* 131, no. 20 (October 1, 2014).

3. Bishops' Committee on Priestly Life and Ministry, *Fulfilled in Your Hearing: The Homily in the Sunday Assembly* (Washington, DC: United States Conference of Catholic Bishops, 1982), 10, emphasis added.

Chapter 8

1. Ralph Waldo Emerson, "The Divinity School Address (1838)," in *Ralph Waldo Emerson: Selected Essays, Lectures, and Poems*, ed. Robert D. Richardson Jr., 118 (New York: Random House, 2006), emphasis added.

2. See the rite for the Ordination of a Deacon (24).